MEMORIES

W. J. LINTON

LONDON

LAWRENCE AND BULLEN

16 HENRIETTA STREET, COVENT GARDEN, W.C.

1895

CONTENTS

iv CONTENTS

PAGE

RECOLLECTIONS

RECOLLECTIONS

CHAPTER I

Earliest Recollections; Stratford; Death of George III.; Queen Caroline; Hone and Cruikshank; Press Gangs; State Lotteries; Copper Coinage; Cheap Illustrated Serials; Scott's Poems and Novels; School Days; Wanstead House.

SOME vague remembrance I still have of the house in which I was born (December 7, 1812) and in which I lived till I was five years old: one of a row of private houses, "Ireland's Row" in the Mile-End Road, at the east end of London, close to Charrington's brewery, — a brewery I believe still prosperously existing. The house was in the parish of Stepney, the parish for all folk born at sea. My real recollections begin with 1820, the year in which George III. ceased to be nominal king of England. My family was then living at Stratford, some four miles out of what was distinctly London in those days: not Chaucer's "Stratford atte Bowe," where the prioress learned French (which is now only Bow), but a continuation distinguished of old as Long Stratford, one of the fords for folk to "dance over my Lady Lea," fords bridged over in my time by, I think, four bridges between Old Bow Church and Stratford proper, now a busy railroad centre then a straggling hamlet of the parish of West Ham, where in old time had been an abbey, and connected with it one of the largest and handsomest churches in England. Early in 1820 I was one evening walking with my father in our garden, a garden in which we showed with pride two almost unknown vegetables, rhubarb (American " pie-plant ") and sea-kail, when we heard the far sound of a deep-toned bell. It was the great bell of St. Paul's Cathedral, only used on the most solemn of State occasions. My father spoke : " The old king is dead."

Next I recollect being in the City, on a visit to some relations, and seeing daily the processions of the city companies (the old-time guilds) passing through the streets with banners and bands of music on their way westward to Hammersmith to present their loyal addresses to Queen Caroline, who, denied her place at court, was there living. For her, if only out of censorious disrespect for the royal husband who rejected her, public sympathy was very strongly evoked. It did not even need her acquittal by the packed and partial tribunal to which she was shamefully dragged by the sovereign profligate to make all that was liberal in England take part with her against him. The queen's cause was also taken advantage of as an anti-governmental policy, calling forth William Hone's political pasquinades, in illustration of which the genius of George

Cruikshank first made its appearance. Shelley's *Œdipus Tyrannus* (Swellfoot the Tyrant, alias gouty George IV.) had its impulse in the same conflict. My father was what was then called "a Queen's Man," and of course took in Hone's pamphlets, — *The House that Jack built*, *The Man in the Moon*, *The Political Showman*, *The Queen's Matrimonial Ladder*, and several others. Some of them, relics of old days, are before me now; fierce but clever, the cuts by Cruikshank not unworthy of his after fame. I can not charge my memory with any observation of them in that childish period of my life; but I must have seen them whether then interested or not.

Not long afterwards was the queen's funeral: on the 7th of June in that year 1820. It was said that she died heart-broken at her disappointment in not being able to obtain admittance to Westminster Abbey, to there insist on her right of coronation as undivorced queen. Refusing her even a grave in England, her body was ordered to be conveyed to Brunswick to be buried there among her own kinfolk. An attempt was made to smuggle the removal through the by-streets of London, but the people barred the way and forced the *cortège* through the principal thoroughfares. Two, there may have been three, mourning coaches, escorted by a few mud-bespattered horse-guards, the "Oxford Blues," formed the funeral procession as it passed through Stratford, passing my father's door, on the way to the port of Harwich. It was the shabbiest notable funeral I ever saw. Very different had been the funeral of Nelson, on which occasion my father as a volunteer kept on Ludgate Hill the way of the solemn procession to St. Paul's, where under the central dome the greatest English admiral since Blake was buried with the utmost honour that could be rendered to the victorious and heroic sailor. Yet even in those days of naval glory, and for many years after, the "common sailor" was arbitrarily and forcibly impressed into the service. I have heard my father tell of the butchers of Whitechapel (an East London street of butchers' shops) turning out armed with their long knives to resist the cutlasses of the press-gangs, who called all fish which they could haul into their nets.

Some few years later than 1820, and for many years earlier, there was the demoralising craze of State lotteries. The contractors for the sale of tickets competed furiously, touting in the streets by thrusting their circulars into the hands of the passengers, rich or poor, old or young. Boy-like, I was pleased to collect these lottery bills, many of them pictorial, well-drawn, and fairly engraved. I believe that Branston, the wood-engraver, Bewick's contemporary, and, as an engraver, his worthy rival, coming from Bath to London in 1799, had his first employment on the cuts of these bills. I think this lottery mania did not outlast my boyhood. Another of my boyish collections was of the remains of a copper coinage of the time of the war against Napoleon, when money was so scarce that " brass buttons passed current," and large manufacturers coined copper " tokens " for the use of their workmen, of course only in their mutual dealings. Some of these tokens were admirably designed and executed, and I had a large number of them.

Of school-days, three years under the Rev. Dr. Burford at Stratford, there is not much to say. They were the first days of cheap, sometimes illustrated, serial publications: the *Portfolio*, a harmless paper, — the respectable *Mirror*, published by Limbird in the Strand, and edited, if not at first, yet later, by John Timbs, afterwards editor of the *Illustrated London News*, — *Endless Entertainment*, *Legends of Horror*, the *Newgate Calendar*, and others: affording much amusement, if not very valuable instruction, to the young. Lord Brougham's Society " for the Diffusion of Useful Knowledge " had not yet glimmered above the horizon, and the Messrs. Chambers were not. Among my early readings were Scott's *Lady of the Lake, Marmion, Rokeby*, and the *Lord of the Isles*, in the first grand quarto editions; books given me to heighten my seat as I wrote my Latin exercises at home; books in lonely opportunities to be lifted from under me for the pleasanter reading. After a serious illness I read in bed some of Scott's novels, one of the volumes of *Rob Roy* in manuscript, page for page written out by Mr. Crick, the Stratford Circulating Librarian, to make good the set of three volumes sold at a guinea and a half, the usual price of novels before the advent of Mudie.

A very quiet village was Stratford then, its lower parts periodically overflowed by the Lea waters. Our basement kitchen might have three feet of flood in it. I have seen the ground floor of the Blue Boar Inn under water to nearly the edge of the table-tops. People living on the marshes could at such times only leave or get to their houses by boats; and in one part of the London road, the great high-way out of London eastward, the road at such times would be impassable for foot-passengers.

Between two and three miles from Stratford, bordering upon Epping — more properly Hainault — Forest, which then extended from Wanstead and Walthamstow through Woodford and Loughton to Epping, was Wanstead Park, the property of Tylney Long Pole Wellesley (I trust I have the names correctly), a nephew of the Duke of Wellington, and one of the fastest of the fast livers of that gorgeous Georgian era. The park, with its noble avenues of trees, its lake, and heronry, was a favourite resort of us school-boys on half-holidays. Wanstead House, in the park, said to be nearly if not quite the largest private house in England, I saw but once, a magnificent building well worthy of the Earl of Leicester, and to have had Queen Elizabeth as guest. Here Sir Philip Sidney wrote his masque, the *Lady of the May*, on occasion of Her Majesty's visit in 1578. Here, too, during a season of her displeasure, Sir Walter Raleigh seems to have been rusticated, if we may attribute to him the " Hermit's Song," in one of Dowland's *Song-Books*. A lovely place was the park till most of the trees were cut down, and a right princely mansion was Wanstead House, despoiled to pay a gambler's debts.

In these school-days but one small incident may bear recalling : our school's excitement at hearing of a new pupil at a rival establishment in Stratford, in the person of a son of Fauntleroy, the banker recently hanged for forgery.

CHAPTER II

Apprenticeship; Dulwich College; The Picture Gallery; The Cruik-
shanks; Hood; Henry Hunt; Old London Bridge; City Sights;
Jonathan Wooler; Richard Carlile; Popular Grievances; Fairs.

IN 1828, having taken lessons in some sort of
drawing, and therefore being fondly supposed to
have an artistic inclination, I was apprenticed
to Mr. George Wilmot Bonner, wood-engraver, a
nephew and pupil of Branston, and went to live
with the Bonner family for six years at Kennington,
a suburb of London on the Surrey side. Bonner was
a clever artist, and a good master, making his pupils
learn and do everything connected with their work,
even to sawing up a box-wood log and planing and
smoothing the rounds of wood to fit them to receive
the drawings. For these we might also sometimes
have to make the sketches and draw them on the
wood for our own engraving. It was good artistic
training. I recollect being sent up the Thames side
to sketch the "Red House" at Battersea (a noted
house for matches of pigeon-shooting) and the old
wooden bridges between Battersea and Chelsea (only
lately removed) and between Putney and Fulham.
In that time of learning, too, I worked occasionally
in the fifteenth century mode of wood-work, with
a knife instead of a graver, on cuts for placards for

8

Ducrow, the manager of Astley's Amphitheatre, the one horse-circus in London, in the Westminster-Bridge Road.

From our workroom window at the back and top of No. 12 Canterbury Row, Kennington, we looked over gardens and fields to the Surrey Zoological Gardens, to which the menagerie of Exeter Change in the Strand was about that time removed. The Surrey Gardens during these my 'prentice days had been laid out and opened as a rival to the Zoological Gardens in the Regent's Park.

From Kennington through Camberwell to Dulwich was then a pleasant walk, after passing Camberwell through country fields, a walk I often took, as I had the fortune to be acquainted with one of the Fellows of Dulwich College, and so was sometimes allowed to spend a Sunday there, rambling in the large College garden, or for hours alone in the most pleasant of picture-galleries attached to the College. The College had been founded and endowed by Edward Alleyn, an actor of Elizabethan days, as an almshouse for six poor bachelor curates of the Church of England: the master and warden to be always of the same name as the founder. At the time I went there, this much-abused "charity" was ground-landlord of more than a mile every way from the College; and, as the letter of the founder's will was still the only rule, the master, warden, and other four "poor curates" lived in clover. One of them held also two livings somewhere in the country, with perhaps two poor curates to do his duty there. Under the Fellows' private rooms dwelt, serving them as janitors, as many poor men, whose ordered pittance had not increased with the property; and a sort of free school for a few village boys was also kept up. Dining together in the common hall, when they preferred that to their own luxurious chambers, these Fellows fared sumptuously, waited on like princes. There was "divine service" on Sundays in the College chapel (adorned with a large picture by Giulio Romano), one or other of the Fellows officiating, one as organist; but else the College was but a palace of drones. Since then, parliamentary interference has, in this as in many other like cases, compelled a more reasonable application of the funds of the endowment. I could even at the time of my visiting perceive the wrongfulness of the abuse; but as a visitor I cared mainly, perhaps only, for the beautiful picture-gallery, with its Murillos and Rembrandts, a Titian, a Guido, a Wouvermans, a Gainsborough, a Reynolds (the places in which they hung I can still remember), and many more, all of which I generally had quite to myself except for a few minutes when noticeable visitors coming out of the chapel were shown round. The gallery is still there, one of the sights for strangers in London.

Not many men of note came within my vision during these my 'prentice days. One was Robert Cruikshank, who made drawings for Cumberland's

British Theatre, as new plays came out at the theatres. The drawings were always engraved by Bonner. The many volumes of plays were the principal part of the small library accessible to me. Robert Cruikshank was far from being the equal of his famous brother; but, being the elder, claimed the right of being *Mister* Cruikshank; and George had to assert himself as artistically the "real Simon Pure," an assertion afterwards mistaken for a statement that it was his real name and Cruikshank a pseudonym: so the reader is gravely informed in a German biographical dictionary, the biographer only too ready to grasp at every information.

Hood I saw at his chambers in the Adelphi when I went to fetch his drawings for his *Comic Annual,* queer pen-and-ink drawings to be cut in fac-simile, some by myself. I recall him only as a spare man of fair stature, grave but not ungenial. But I most regarded his tools. Beside pencil and pen there lay on his desk an old graver, a reminiscence of his early time as an engraver in copper, a penknife, and a nail, with which it appeared he cut or scraped out any wrong line in his drawing. One other notable man I once saw was Henry Hunt, "the radical," with a white chimney-pot hat, his obnoxious sign of radicalism, in a waggon on his way to take the chair at a political meeting on Kennington Common, a great place for public meetings until prudently converted into a "park" for the more innocent amusement of the populace.

A thing to be remembered was the first passing over New London Bridge, between Southwark ("the Borough") and the City (I mind not the exact date of its building — between 1828 and 1831), and looking down on the old bridge by the side of the new and many feet below it, the old bridge with its wide wooden abutments to the piers, and on each side of the roadway the half-cupola niches with seats, in which one could hear a conversation in the niche on the opposite side, the like of what was to be heard in the "Whispering Gallery" round the inside of the dome of St. Paul's Cathedral. Another City wonder, still happily existing, outliving Temple Bar, the last of the City Gates, was the Giant Gog, with his fellow-giant Magog, standing in Guildhall, each in a high niche, from which, according to the veracious legend, they came down to dinner every day when they heard the clock strike one. In the Guildhall too, so I was informed, was a pillar with a cavity called "Little Ease," in which refractory apprentices were confined. City of London apprentices, it must be understood, of which I was one, being as matter of form "bound" to an elder half-brother, to entitle me to the freedom of the Scriveners' Company (the Guild to which Milton belonged) after due years of nominal service. Never wanting to open a shop in the City precincts, I never took up my "freedom." Of course I was acquainted with the bas-relief of a boy on a basket, marking the highest ground in London, in Pannier Alley, close by St. Paul's; and with "London Stone," some three feet of the top of which is, I believe, still visible near the Cannon Street Railway Station, the stone really some twenty feet high, the ground raised since the old Romans set it on their Watling Street, their highway through the country. I may note also yet another City wonder, since removed, in front of old St. Dunstan's Church in Fleet Street; two life-sized figures which, one on each side of a bell, struck the hours. Not very far from opposite, about that time, or it may have been later, I think at the corner of Bouverie Street, was Richard Carlile's shop, over which, in an upper window, stood two life-sized figures — "the Devil and a Bishop," cheek by jowl, scandalising the pious passers-by. Carlile had followed in the wake of Jonathan Wooler (editor of the *Black Dwarf*) and Hone, as publisher of proscribed books, Palmer's *Principles of Nature*, Paine's *Age of Reason*; and other such, for which wickedness he suffered under different sentences nine years of imprisonment. It was the heyday of governmental prosecutions for "seditious" speaking or publishing and "blasphemy," in which the Government was not always successful. On one occasion Carlile took advantage of the law that a full report of a trial was permissible, and read in his defence the whole of Paine's *Age of Reason*; so legally procuring repetition of the offence for which he was indicted, and for which he was sentenced to three years' imprisonment in Dorchester Gaol.

Popular objections to things as they were had not much of "sweetness and light," but were sometimes as harsh and unseemly as their provocation. Two low fellows parading London streets of an evening as parson and clerk, mouthing out a ribald parody of the "Form of Common Prayer," did not betoken much popular respect for either Church or State; but there was ground for bitter feeling and disrespect among the lower orders, kept lower, when Dorchester labourers were imprisoned for too plainly avowed discontent at four shillings a week as the support for a family; when men were sent to prison for "unlawfully assembling on a Sunday;" when for the mere selling of an unstamped newspaper men and women were also punished with incarceration. But of this I shall have to speak when I tell of my friends Watson and Hetherington. As an apprentice I might not take part in any public matter; but I wore the badge of the National Association at the passing of the Reform Bill, and had learned to feel an interest in public affairs.

These were days of yearly fairs: Bow Fair, where while yet a child I was taken, to be disgusted with the ugliness of wax-work; Camberwell Fair, to which I went in 'prentice time; and "Bartlemy" (Bartholomew) Fair, held near St. Bartholomew's Hospital, in Smithfield: permitted gatherings these of unruly crowds, for whom was provided the roughest kind of amusement, theatrical and other, coarse, vulgar, and obscene, to suit the lowest tastes. I can not recollect how it was that one night, after my apprenticeship, I found myself in a low public house near Smithfield, thence following a riotous crowd which at midnight proceeded, shouting and knocking at doors, to "proclaim the Fair" (to be opened next day by proclamation of the lord mayor) as a proceeding necessary to maintain the charter.

All these fairs, with many more throughout the country, were held by charters of different kings, and in old days had met conveniences of trade; becoming, however, at last mere disorderly nuisances, a disgrace to even the rough "civilisation" of the early part of the nineteenth century. Bartholomew Fair, in the heart of the City, was the worst of these, unless indeed its grossnesses of vice could have been surpassed by those of Greenwich, held in Greenwich Park behind the Sailors' Hospital, — of which grossnesses old Francis Place (the radical Westminster tailor whose political influence placed Burdett and Hobhouse in Parliament) told me tales, of the days when he was young and manners were yet more rough and indecent.

CHAPTER III

Church Services; Landor; Carlton House; First Perversion; My
First Friend; W. J. Huggins, Marine Painter to William IV.;
Duncan; Wade; Horne.

From my father, the first Englishman of his race
(his father was an Aberdeen ship-carpenter who
settled in London as a builder, with fair pretension
also to be called an architect), I perhaps inherited
some tendency to radicalism; certainly not from
my mother, who, my father not interfering, brought
up myself and a younger brother and two sisters
in the tenets of the Church of England, her utmost
show of tolerance to send us small children on wet
Sundays, when it was not fit for us to walk the
more than a mile to our parish church at West
Ham, to a small Methodist chapel, only a few doors
from home, which we called " Mamma's Little Meeting." I do not remember that she ever went there
with us. Too young to be impressed with the Thirty-
nine Articles, I was none the less endoctrinated in
the Athanasian Creed and the special church services,
of course including those in commemoration of the
" Blessed Martyr," Charles I., and the happy restoration of his worthy son; and so fairly trained through
all the ceremonials of the church as by law estab-

16

lished. Excellent those commemorative services for the two Charleses if, as Walter Savage Landor observed, each could be changed for the other! After all, though England was not a gainer politically or morally by the accession of her easy-going crowned libertine, yet (as even a clergyman of the Established Church, J. Woodfall Ebsworth, the good vicar of Molash, Kent, once remarked to me) he had one saving grace, " he was not such a liar as his father." Perhaps to teach me some additional reverence for the contemporary loyalty, which, mean as it was, was not without blind loyal worshipers, I was once taken by a family friend, who had been a page of the Prince Regent, to see the state apartments in Carlton House, which had been one of the Regent's palaces, then standing on the side of St. James' Park, at the foot of Waterloo Place, where now are the steps into the park and the column on which is the statue of the Duke of York, the king's brother, so elevated, it was wickedly said, " to be out of the reach of his creditors."

My first perversion may have come from a fellow-engraver, a young man from Stockton-on-Tees, who sat beside me during the last two years of my apprenticeship, and who was what, in those days, was not reputable — that is, he was an Unitarian, and so " not a Christian " in the estimation of the pious according to law. There was nothing else against him, and he showed considerable talent as an engraver. But I owed more of free thought to a

c

friend a few years older than myself, a stock-broker's clerk and also organist at two city churches,
with whom, between the services, at our lunch in an
else untenanted office, I read Voltaire's *Philosophical
Dictionary.* He, I suppose, would have been called
worse than Unitarian, an " infidel." Certainly a
non-conformist, though in no way aggressive or ob-
trusive; but to be such, however inoffensively, was
enough for him to be shut from his respectable
father's house, and to have his mother and sisters
forbidden to speak to him if by chance they met
him in the street. To me, in my recollection of
him, he seems to have been the most beautifully
natured man I have ever known, almost womanly
in his delicacy of aspect and gentleness of manner,
yet with a keen masculine intellect and firmness of
character and will. Opposed and hindered in every
way by his father, — not a bad man, but a bigot, —
he at last emigrated to Australia, as a clerk in one
of the first Australian banks. There he died. He
was more than a brother to me, and his memory is
still very dear. My first acquaintance with him
was near the end of my apprenticeship. I knew
him as the friend of Edward Duncan, the talented
water-colour painter, at that time an aqua-tint engraver, engraving portraits of horses and of ships,
from paintings by his father-in-law, W. J. Huggins,
Marine Painter to his Majesty King William IV.
Very different the artist's position at that time from
what it has become since. Huggins lived where no

fairly successful artist would think of living now, in Leadenhall Street, not far from opposite to the East India House, in a narrow house, only two small rooms on a floor, the ground floor a shop, kept by his son for the sale of engravings from paintings by the father, of portraits of ships, and where they could be seen by East India captains, for whom, in general, they were painted. Above the shop were parlour and kitchen; over them the bedrooms, and at top the painting-room, where the painter, a jolly, fat, good-natured fellow, who had been ship's cook in the same vessel in which Stanfield was a cabin-boy, smoked his pipe and drank his all-water grog, of which he would jocosely offer a share to his visitors; and where, on the drugget flooring of the room, he would chalk the positions of the several vessels in a naval action. For he was not a mere ship-portrait painter, but did higher things, painted for the king three large pictures of the Battle of Navarino, which his Marine Majesty would come to see in progress, for all the shop and the climb up steep and narrow stairs. Huggins was a kind and instructive friend to me, and his son-in-law, Edward Duncan, was my good friend for many after years, until his death.

Toward the close of my apprenticeship, I became acquainted with Thomas Wade and his friend Richard Hengist Horne. Wade, the author of a volume of thoughtful and imaginative poems, *Mundi et Cordis Carmina*, published in 1835, of a play, *The Jew of Arragon*, brought out by Charles Kemble (in which

Fanny Kemble, afterwards Mrs. Butler, played the heroine), and of other poems. He (Wade) should have made a high mark in literature, but under pressure of some money difficulties, betook himself to Jersey, a sort of debtors' Alsatia in those days, and there obtained a living by editing a weekly newspaper. There he died, leaving MSS. of verse, in the hands of Mr. Buxton Forman, yet unpublished.

Horne, in 1835, had already published his fine tragedy of *Cosmo de' Medici*, in five acts, and *The Death of Marlowe*, in one act, works with more of the vigorous character and high poetic quality of the Elizabethan dramatists than anything that has been written since the Elizabethan days. Somewhat later he brought out a noble epic poem, *Orion*, which, in a freak to prove that the age did not care for poetry, he issued at the price of one farthing. His publisher would not let me have a second farthing's worth. He proved his case: the sale was small. I think years afterwards there might have been some additional small demand for the book when published at five shillings. A prose work, — an *Exposition of the False Medium, the Barriers between Men of Genius and the Public,* — a fierce onslaught on the publishers' Reader and the Reviewers, did not help him to a too friendly critical appreciation. And his work was very unequal. A *Life of Napoleon* was hardly more than a wordy enlargement of that by Hazlitt; and an imaginary

Life of Van Amburg, the Lion-Tamer, and papers unsigned in the *Monthly Repository* under the editorship of W. J. Fox, and for a short time of Leigh Hunt, only showed his clever versatility. *Gregory VII.*, a five-act tragedy, deserved a lofty place; but very much of later work, despite notable exceptions, did not reach the same height. A man of indubitable genius, he yet wanted that one element of genius, humour. Still he merited far more than he had of contemporary appreciation, and very much of his verse may rank with the very best of that of the nineteenth century poets. A remarkable man also in other respects; small in stature, but with a grand head, beautiful in young days when he was a cadet at Woolwich, serving afterwards in the war for Mexican independence, for which service he, up to the time of his death, drew a small annuity; he was also one of the sub-commissioners appointed to inquire into the condition of women and children in our mines, horrible enough to demand inquiry; he lectured, in 1847, on Italy, when, with Mazzini's aid, the *People's International League* strove to stir the public mind in favour of Italian freedom; had command later, when in Australia (where he went with William Howitt), of the escort of gold from the mines; and also sat in the Australian legislature. Coming back to England after several years, he continued to write, sometimes with his old vigour; his last work, *Sithron the Star-stricken*, worthy of his best days.

He was a musician, played well on the guitar, and sang well. I was in England at the end of 1882, and during the following year, and half of 1884; and, our acquaintanceship resumed, spent many evenings with the old man at his lodgings in Northumberland Street, Marylebone. Through the two winters he would cook our dinner at the stove in his sitting-room, priding himself on his cooking (he was very much of an epicure, an epicurean in his life), and we ate on what room was left by books and letters on a little round table before the fire. He had always good wine, supplied by an admiring friend, and we sat and talked of books or of his Australian life. He was proud of showing how strong, in spite of his years (his dated with the century), his physique still was; and one evening he showed me his bare foot, that I might see he was really web-footed. He had taken several prizes for swimming; on one occasion had been thrown into the water hands and feet tied, to prove that merely touching the end of a straw could keep a man afloat, — of course he did not need the straw. After reaching the "threescore years and ten," he leaped from the pier at Eastbourne to give a lesson in swimming. One evening I found him not in his usual spirits. He had been dining out the evening before, and I thought there had been some imprudent excess. A day or two later he was in bed with gastric fever, and only recovered sufficiently to go for change of air to the sea at Margate, where after a few days he died. We buried the old man there, though it had been his wish to be laid near Charles Lamb at Edmonton. I am not sure that he had known Lamb, though it may have been. Hazlitt he had known, and, I believe, had nursed in his last sickness. I always think of Horne as one who ought to have been great, he came so near it in his work, in the greatness and nobility of his best writings.

CHAPTER IV

W. J. Fox; Southwood Smith; Eliza Flower; Sarah Flower Adams;
W. B. Adams; Watson; Hetherington; *The Poor Man's Guardian;* Movement for a Free Press; Heywood; Moore; Hibbert.

IN 1837, Wade was living, with his mother and sisters, in Great Quebec Street, Montague Square. He had just given up editing the *Bell's New Weekly Messenger*, a liberal newspaper. On Sunday evenings he gave receptions, when there would be music by Mrs. Bridgman (distinguished as a fine pianiste, afterwards the wife of Wade), and where I would meet Horne, Douglas Jerrold, W. J. Fox (the eloquent Unitarian preacher), Dr. Southwood Smith (one of Bentham's executors, and physician to the Jews' and fever hospitals), Margaret Gillies (the miniature painter), and her sister Mary (a writer of the Mary Howitt class, and a most amiable woman), and others. We had good music and, I dare to say, good talk, to which I listened. After this I was a frequent visitor in Fox's house, there becoming acquainted with Eliza Flower, the musical composer, and her sister, the author of the hymn "Nearer, my God! to Thee," the wife of William Bridges Adams, one of our best civil engineers, a man held in high esteem in his profession, and also for his most unselfish and wide philanthropy. He, his wife, and her sister, became my intimate and dearest friends.

Eliza Flower's music, *Hymns and Anthems*, was the music at South Place Chapel, Finsbury, the church of an advanced section of religious Unitarians, the followers of William Johnson Fox, a man whose eloquence drew all the best of the liberal notabilities, — such men as John Stuart Mill and Disraeli — to listen to him. The musical services, too, at the chapel sought a high religious ground, the *Hymns and Anthems* consisting of selections from Scripture and from old divines and poets, set by Eliza Flower to worthy music of notable originality and excellence. Some of the hymns were by Fox himself; others by Sarah Flower Adams, who should also be remembered for a very noble tragic " dramatic poem," *Vivia Perpetua*, of similar subject but very different treatment to Massinger's *Virgin Martyr*. The sisters were two of the most beautiful women of their day, daughters of Benjamin Flower, editor of the *Cambridge Intelligencer*, the earliest of our liberal newspapers. They had been friends of Browning in his young manhood, — the first to recognize and call attention to his genius. To me their friendship, a love as of two elder sisters, too soon to be interrupted by their death (that of Eliza Flower in December, 1846, and of Mrs. Adams in 1848, a year and a half later), was indeed a liberal education. With their love and feeling for music and pictorial art, and their high poetic thought, they were such women in their purity, intelligence, and high-souled enthusiasm, as Shelley might have sung as fitted to redeem a world by their very presence.

Fox ought to have been the leader, as well as a great teacher, of the people. I think he was only prevented by a physique which made him inactive. He was a short, stout man, with a grand head and fine eyes,— the most poetic and rich-languaged of all great speakers I have heard, only not so classic as Wendell Phillips. He was afterwards Member of Parliament for Oldham. He was also, in private, a good verse-improvisatore.

I owed very much to the influence of Fox. Before I knew him personally, hearing lectures by him, and reading Shelley's *Queen Mab* and Lamennais' *Words of a Believer* (*Paroles d'un Croyant*), had stirred me with the passion of Reform. Passing to the city from the Lower Road, Islington, where, the days of pupilage over, I was living in 1835–6, I would look into a bookseller's shop, a few doors from Bunhill Fields (John Bunyan's burial-place), in the City Road, Finsbury, to buy Roebuck's *Pamphlets* (parliamentary critiques), or Volney's *Ruins of Empire* and *Lectures on History*, or Frances Wright's *Few Days at Athens*, or the works of Godwin, Paine, or Robert Dale Owen: all of them the neat and cheap publications of James Watson, in 1835 just out of prison for selling an unstamped newspaper, — a man whose evident sin-

:erity and quiet earnestness led me into conversation :oncerning the books he sold, and on other matters also. With him began my first acquaintance with Chartism, a movement of no small importance, however little now is thought or known of it, which arose out of the action of Henry Hetherington, a London printer. His fight for a free press should first be spoken of.

In 1831, and after, with the " reforming " Whigs in power, it still remained illegal, so declared by the government administrators, to give political knowledge to the people : illegal *ipso facto*, to render the giving impossible. There was a four-penny stamp on every periodical publication that gave news. Caution money was required before a newspaper could be issued, in order that, in case of conviction for anything which could be construed as offensive to the government, the fine might be at hand. There was also a tax upon every advertisement, and a duty upon paper. To contend against such a state of things, this printer Hetherington, after several vain attempts to evade the law, began the publication of the *Poor Man's Guardian*, a weekly paper for the people, " established contrary to law, which will contain (in the words of the prohibitory Act, here in italic) *news, intelligence, occurrences, and remarks and observations thereon, tending* decidedly *to excite hatred and contempt of the government and constitution of* the tyranny *of this country as by law established, and also to vilify* the abuses *of religion;* and will be *printed in the United Kingdom for sale and published periodically* (every Saturday) *at intervals not exceeding twenty-six days,* and *not exceeding two sheets ;* and will be published *for a less sum than sixpence* (to wit, the sum of ONE PENNY) *exclusive of the duty imposed by the* 38 *Geo. III., cap.* 78, *and* 60 *Geo. III., c.* 9, or any other acts whatsoever."

For selling a single copy of such a paper, proof given before a magistrate was deemed to be sufficient for conviction ; and during three years and a half, more than five hundred men and women were under magisterial sentences imprisoned for various periods ; Hetherington himself twice for six months. Still he persevered, and at last succeeded in forcing a trial in the Court of Exchequer before Lord Lyndhurst and a special jury, when the *Guardian* was declared to be a " strictly legal publication." Of course there was no redress for the more than five hundred persons who had suffered illegally.

Among the imprisoned was Abel Heywood, a bookseller of Manchester and wholesale agent for the *Guardian,* so a fair target for prosecution. He took his prison degree, paid his fines, and went on selling the paper. Then the authorities seized the papers in the hands of the carriers, and various devices had to be resorted to in order that they might circulate in safety. Some packed with shoes, some with chests of tea, some otherwise, the prohibited goods were sent through the country, and their sale was continued until the reduction of the duty, as was expected, destroyed their monopoly of cheapness. But by this time the *Guardian* had been made the foundation of a business, which Heywood's ability and perseverance enlarged, until he, denounced in these early days as "seditious," became, without change of principles or political conduct, an influential and well-to-do citizen, mayor of Manchester, and might have represented Manchester in Parliament had he cared to do so. To his second wife, a woman of some wealth, we owe the erection in Manchester of the first statue of Oliver Cromwell.

Watson, Hetherington's closest friend, the son of a Yorkshire day-labourer, his mother a very intelligent and energetic woman, had his three prison services: the first of twelve months for selling Palmer's *Principles of Nature* in Carlile's shop (he had come to London from Malton in Yorkshire to volunteer as shopman for Carlile, Carlile and his wife being both in prison, she under a two years' sentence), then twice, six months each time, for selling the *Guardian*. Such had been English freedom under the infamous Castlereagh administration in the reign of George IV., and such it remained under liberal Whig rule after the passing of the Reform Bill, a measure only meaned, in later words of Richard Cobden, to "garrison our present institutions" against the rising democracy.

The popularity of the cheap unstamped papers injuring the sale of the stamped higher-priced, compelled them also to join in the agitation against the stamp; and the consequence of their coöperation was the reduction of the tax from fourpence to one penny, which Mr. Hume rightly called the worst penny of the lot. This reduction, as anticipated, ruined the unstamped. But the reduction did not stop the agitation. The " Society for the Repeal of all the Taxes on Knowledge" took up the question, and after thirteen years of incessant action (the committee met 473 times) forced the government to give up not only the remaining penny stamp on every paper, but also the tax on advertisements and that on the manufacture of paper. Most active in this later movement was the indefatigable chairman, Richard Moore, a wood-carver, who was happily married to a niece of Watson, and who was in close fellowship with Watson in all his public life. A man singularly modest and quietly persistent was Moore, for more than forty years among the foremost in all the liberal movements of that time; a leading elector in the most radical borough of Finsbury, returning Wakley and Duncombe to Parliament, in active sympathy with the cause of Poland and that of Italy, and enjoying the esteem and friendship of leading politicians, of those even whose views were not so far-going as his own. It was fairly written of him at his death in 1878, that " all the prominent English Radicals and liberal Exiles he could reckon among his friends . . . the purity of his life was only equalled by his disinterestedness . . . there was something singularly earnest, gentle, and chivalrous in his character." This man I am proud to speak of as my friend.

Another man, before I leave the story of the un-stamped, must not be left unmentioned, though I only knew him by report: Julian Hibbert, the treas-urer and "chief prop" of the Victim Fund during the battle for the *Poor Man's Guardian*. For the victims of the government prosecutions were not left uncared for. Hibbert was, I believe, brought up as a Catholic, a man of "good family," education, and some wealth, who identified himself with the political and free-thinking movements which had then to encounter disrepute and obloquy, — a man whose portrait (now before me) reminds me of Shelley, who seems, indeed, to have been a prose Shelley, with the same gentleness of nature and chivalrous zeal against wrong. He died in 1834.

CHAPTER V

The People's Charter; Major Cartwright; The London Working Men's Association; Crown and Anchor Conference; The Chartist Convention; O'Connor; Spies; *The Odd Fellow;* Hetherington; Watson.

THE "People's Charter" was an endeavour to carry out the principles of Major John Cartwright, who, born in 1740 and dying in 1824, is noteworthy, in the words beneath his statue in Burton Crescent, London, as "the firm, consistent, and persevering advocate of universal suffrage," and reform in Parliament: principles which, though they had been accepted, were not insisted on by Earl Grey in his Reform Bill. The immediate movement for the Charter grew out of a document prepared by Hetherington in 1831, which originated the "National Union of the Working Classes," — "to collect and organise a peaceful and open expression of public opinion" (so superseding the secret societies of the time), "and to obtain an effectual reform in Parliament," instead of the partial reform which was all that was attainable by the Whig Reform Bill. The National Union of the Working Classes was, after much good educational work, disturbed, and, to a great extent, displaced by the trades unions; but a section still sought to continue the political action by the formation in

1836 of the "London Working Men's Association," an association whose published addresses called forth the admiration of even so fastidious a literary critic as Leigh Hunt. In February, 1837, this association convened a public meeting at the Crown and Anchor Tavern in the Strand, out-door meetings being illegal and two attempts having been stopped by the Reform Government. A petition to the House of Commons for universal suffrage and better ordering of elections, adopted at that meeting, was placed in the hands of John Arthur Roebuck, M. P. for Sheffield, for presentation to the House; and the association towards its support requested a conference with those members of the reformed House who professed liberal principles. Eight answered: Colonel Perronet Thompson, Joseph Hume, Charles Hindley, Daniel O'Connell, Dr. Bowring, John Temple Leader, William Sherman Crawford, and Benjamin Hawes; all, except Hawes, after two nights' discussion, accepting the principles of the association. O'Connell dodged, had a scheme of his own, but, that not approved of, agreed to the course of the association, not honestly, as afterwards appeared.

Resolutions were adopted, pledging the above-named members, Hawes excepted, to support the petition to be presented by Roebuck, and to support and vote for a bill to be brought into the House of Commons " embodying the principles of universal suffrage, equal representation, free selection of representatives without reference to property, the ballot, and

D

short Parliaments of fixed duration, the limit not to exceed three years"; and appointing a committee of twelve to draw up the bill. The committee consisted of six Members of Parliament, — Thompson, Crawford, Leader, Roebuck, Hindley, and O'Connell; and six members of the Working Men's Association, — Henry Hetherington, John Cleave, James Watson (three booksellers), Richard Moore (carver), William Lovett (cabinet-maker), and Henry Vincent (journeyman printer). Roebuck and Lovett were to draft the bill; but, owing to Roebuck's parliamentary engagements, the work was really done by Lovett, with Roebuck's legal advice. This was the "People's Charter," first published on the 8th of May, 1838, accepted at large public meetings in Glasgow and Birmingham, and in London at an important public meeting in Palace Yard, Westminster, called by the high bailiff on the requisition of a large number of influential citizens. One of the speakers I saw and heard at this meeting was Ebenezer Elliott, the "Corn-Law Rhymer."

A Convention of fifty-five persons, elected by show of hands at public meetings throughout the country of, it was said, three millions of persons, sat in London in the following year, to consider of the means to obtain the charter; and, having placed a petition with 1,228,000 signatures in the hands of Mr. Atwood, M. P. for Birmingham, for presentation to Parliament, transferred their sittings to Birmingham, and then dispersed to hold meetings throughout the country. The petition was presented and rejected by the Reformed House of Commons, by 235 votes against 46. Thereupon followed hot and angry talk, chiefly by Feargus O'Connor (formerly a follower of O'Connell), who, in his *Northern Star*, a newspaper published at Leeds, and assuming to be the organ of the Chartists (in reality only of the unwiser section who prided themselves on the advocacy of physical force), broke up the coherence and the *morale* of the party and, aided by arbitrary arrests and imprisonments for " seditious " speaking, much of it provoked by government spies, caused at last an insane attempt at insurrection in South Wales. After that came disheartening, lukewarmness, with intermittent bluster, indifference, and so an end to all hopes of popular success.

How spies were employed to worm themselves into the Chartist movement, to incite to outbreaks or at least to intemperate language which the Government could construe as seditious, was exposed before Parliament by Cobbett, while Member for Oldham. He proved that one Popay and other spies were employed by the police with the knowledge of the Government, and paid out of the Secret Service money. This Popay joined the Union of the Working Classes, winning confidence by his professions and activity, attending the class meetings in order to report them, suggesting and even drawing up resolutions of a violent character, and urging the procuring of arms with a view to open rebellion. An extract from Cobbett's report of the evidence, laid before the Select Committee of the House of Commons, will give some idea of the man and of the system.

"Your Committee request the House first to cast their eyes over the ten months' deeds of this most indefatigable and unrelenting spy; to survey the circle of his exploits from the Borough Town Hall to Blackheath, and from Copenhagen House to Finsbury Square; to behold him dancing with the wife of the man whom he had denounced in his reports, and, standing on a tomb-stone, writing down and then reporting the words uttered over the grave of a departed reformer (Thelwall's speech at Hardy's grave in Bunhill Fields burial-ground); to trace him going from meeting to meeting, and from group to group, collecting matter for accusation in the night, and going regularly in the morning bearing the fruits of his perfidy to his immediate employer, to be by him conveyed to the Government; to follow him into the houses of John B. Young and Mr. Sturgis, and there see his wife and children relieved and fed and warmed and cherished, and then look at one of his written reports and see him describe Young's Union class as armed to a man, and at another see him describe Mr. Sturgis as the teacher of a doctrine that 'fitted man for the worst offences'; and see Lord Melbourne writing on the back of this report that 'it is not unimportant and ought not to be lost sight of.' . . . Your Committee request the House to cast their eyes over these ten months of the life of this man, and then consider whether it is possible for a Government to preserve the affections of a frank and confiding people, unless it at once, in the most unequivocal manner, give proof of its resolution to put an end, and forever, to a system which could have created such a monster in human shape."

Under such a system it could be no matter for wonder, that for hasty, if not intemperate speaking, always "seditious," four hundred and forty-three

" Chartists " were imprisoned for different periods in 1839 and 1840.

Yet that Chartist agitation, mere bootless talk as it may be considered, was the fair outstarting and the sure promise of all political gain which has since accrued to the working classes. And the first movers in it were men worthy to be held in honourable remembrance. Most of them I knew personally, and was in close fellowship with them always. Hetherington, Watson, and Moore, were my intimate friends; Lovett I knew well; Cleave not so well; and Vincent I only recall as an enthusiastic and able speaker, whose outspokenness was not always wise. He paid in prison for the unwisdom.

Hetherington was a leader of men, a ready and effective speaker, plain, pathetic, humorous, or sarcastic, as occasion required; a bold thinker and a good organizer, prompt, energetic, earnest, and devoted. As a printer, publisher, and news-agent, he might have become a rich man, but his time was only too ungrudgingly given to the public service, which he would not neglect even when his attention to it might be at the risk of his own business. I knew him well, for more than a year, from April, 1841, to August, 1842, editing for him one of his unstamped papers, the *Odd Fellow*, so entitled because it chronicled the proceedings of the " Odd Fellows," at that time and since an extensive benefit society. In this paper I wrote weekly political leading articles, much verse, chiefly political, and criticisms of plays, books, etc. Among the criticisms were a laudatory review of Dickens' *Old Curiosity Shop*, and one on the first performance of Gerald Griffin's *Gisippus*, brought out by Macready at Drury Lane Theatre, a production notable not only on account of the play itself, but also for the novel appropriateness of the setting of the drama in its scenery and accessories, such unusual ordering due to Macready, who repeated the same appropriateness, an example to all scenic propriety since, in the production of Leigh Hunt's *Legend of Florence*, a play, though well performed, too refined and purely beautiful for general appreciation. I was present at the first performance of that also.

My editorship bringing me into such constant communication with Hetherington, I was well able to judge of the character of the man. Popular among the better portion of the Chartist party, not unpopular even with those to whose policy and conduct he was opposed, I found him to be one for whom I could not but have a sincere respect and very warm regard.

Watson was of the old Puritan type of our great Cromwellian time, such a man as Ireton, simply wise, serious, and most earnest; a good, not a great speaker, his speeches of few words, but always clear and to the purpose; a brave specimen of the intelligent and honest English workman. I think of him always as a workman, for his life seemed to show that the ideal he had before him was what an English workman ought to be ; and though he kept a bookseller's shop, he was in no sense a tradesman — a buyer and seller merely for gain. His publishing was only of works for the benefit of his fellows. He was a man whom his most violent opponents could not but respect for his integrity and calm, manly self-possession under all circumstances ; essentially a religious man, a believer in duty, though he bowed in neither church nor chapel, and only gave an honestly industrious life for freedom of thought and speech, his whole course a commentary on the words of Milton : "Give me the liberty to know, to utter, and to argue freely according to conscience above all liberties." He was my close and dear friend for thirty-seven years, until his death.

CHAPTER VI

Lovett and Collins; Cooper; Bronterre O'Brien; O'Connor; Outbreak in Wales; Frost; Protest against Death Punishment; Carlyle; Fairfield Festival; Leigh Hunt.

OF Richard Moore, my friend, too, for the like period, I have already written. Lovett was the gentlest of agitators, a mild, peace-loving man, whom nothing but a deep sense of sympathy with and duty toward the wronged could have dragged into public life. His chief ambition, apparent in the later evening of his day when the Chartist movement was at an end, would have been to do good work as an efficient school-teacher. Yet he, too, encountering oppression, had his share of punishment, sentenced, with John Collins, a fellow-member of the Chartist Convention, to twelve months' imprisonment in Warwick gaol for having signed (Lovett as secretary) and printed the resolution of the Convention then sitting at Birmingham (it was only taken to be printed by Collins), a temperate and manly protest of the Convention against a brutal attack by the police upon the people assembled peaceably in their usual place of meeting, the Bull Ring at Birmingham. This police outrage provoked a riot, which was all the Government wanted as giving a colour for farther proceedings. From the 25th of July, 1839, to the same date in 1840, the two Chartists remained in gaol, most harshly treated.

On the 3d of August, 1840, a public dinner, to congratulate the offenders on their liberation, was given at the White Conduit House, Mr. Wakley, surgeon and coroner, the editor of the *Lancet*, and M. P. for Finsbury, in the chair, and his fellow-member, Mr. Duncombe, also present. More than a thousand persons attended. At this dinner I met and was introduced to a tall, stalwart Frenchman, Godfrey Cavaignac, the chief of the French Republicans, the brother of the unrepublican general who put down the Paris insurrection of June, 1848.

Thomas Cooper, the poet-shoemaker, was a man of a very different character from Lovett; impulsive, hot-headed, and, I doubt not, in his early utterances, sufficiently careless of his words to be considered "seditious," and so promoted to two years in prison, where in Spenserian stanzas he wrote his "prison rhyme," the *Purgatory of Suicides*, a long poem, remarkable if only for being produced under prison difficulties, but also as evincing much thoughtful reading, and not without passages of true poetic beauty. When he came out of prison, the rarity of such a performance gave him a certain notoriety and importance. He came to London, and there took an active part in the Chartist movement, more especially in the endeavour at its revival, when new hopes arose with the February days of France. Chartism at an end, he became an itinerant preacher, I think in the Baptist connection. A simple-hearted, good man, quick-tempered and enthusiastic, he was an eloquent orator and a good writer. His *Letters to Working Men* are of excellent sense, and in plain, earnest, vigorous English, reminding one of, and worthy of comparison with, the best writing of Cobbett. His *Autobiography* is a notable book. Kindly natured, though easy to take offence, the offence was soon forgiven. He was trying, on one occasion, to persuade me to join some " League of Universal Brotherhood," when I answered : " Cooper ! I know only two of the Brothers, yourself and Howitt (a man as warm-tempered as Cooper), and I am not tempted to be a third." I once said of him that he would be an excellent coöperator if the *coöper* were in two syllables. It was too severe to fairly characterise the man. He died, very deservedly respected, so late as 1892, in the eighty-seventh year of his age. Among the Chartist crowd, I would also select for notice James Bronterre O'Brien, an Irishman, perhaps the cleverest man of our party, and a forcible speaker.

The Chartist movement was a people's protest against the misgovernment of an oligarchy. It but followed the example set by the middle classes in their struggle for the Reform Bill ; and at first was even more closely within legal limits, superseding by open speech the dangerous growl of secret societies.

But when Feargus O'Connor, a man of probably quite honest intentions, but of little fibre and impolitic, through the influence of the wide circulation of his paper, the *Northern Star*, became prominent as a leader, the course was changed. The *Star* helped and encouraged fierce and foolish talk of what might be done by force. This led, at the close of 1839, to an outbreak in Wales, with the purpose of liberating Vincent from Monmouth gaol, in prison there for too plain speaking: an ill-advised and ill-planned outbreak, easily put down, for which the leader, John Frost (up to that time a man of quiet respectability as a linen-draper, a magistrate, and mayor of Newport), was, with two others, Zephaniah Williams and Jones, sentenced to death. While they were in prison awaiting their trial, I, then living at Woodford, some eight miles from London, had a visit from Watson to tell me that one of the rebels, who had been put in prison chiefly that he might be used as a witness against Frost, had escaped and was then in London, at Hetherington's. Would I give him refuge and take care of him? Of course I would. So he came, little more than a lad (and a nice lad), and stayed with me until the trial was over, not then having much to fear, on account of his youth.

When news came that the death-sentence of the three men was really to be carried out, and that the gallows was being erected, it was in the little sitting-room behind Watson's shop in the City Road that we copied out a petition for reprieve, to which the subscriptions received in not many hours became so numerous that the government was fain to send the announcement of a stay of the death-sentence to Hetherington's more prominent place of business in the Strand, to be there exhibited to allay the popular excitement. The sentence of death was commuted to transportation for life. Frost was allowed after some forty years to return to England. Jones and Williams, I believe, died abroad.

I thought then to make the opportunity available for an influential protest against death-punishment; and consulted Dr. Southwood Smith, Dr. Birkbeck (the founder of the first Mechanics' Institute), and Fox. Fox sent me to Birkbeck for him to draw up the protest. Birkbeck sent me back to Fox. He still hesitating, I wrote the protest myself, and approved by Birkbeck, went on my way, calling first upon Carlyle. I had never seen him, and had no introduction except my purpose. He received me well, talked with me, but would not sign the protest, which included Frost. " No! " he said, " he respected the Quaker principle, but force must be met by force; who took the sword must expect to perish by the sword," or words to that effect. Then he spoke of the men, — " Poor Frost! " and tears were in his eyes; " but I am sorry for him." From him I went to his neighbour, Leigh Hunt, who received me with most kindly warmth and unhesitatingly gave me his signature. Yet as I went away, I thought there was something in the manner of Carlyle's refusal which touched me more closely than even Hunt's prompt acquiescence. There was a deep-heartedness in it, in which I have kept faith, despite all harshnesses of utterance: which, I think, have not justly characterised him. One other thing of later happening may also show his better depth, when not disturbed by dyspepsia. A young German had become a member of a queer society or community, raw vegetarians and else, located at Alcott House, on Ham Common, near Richmond on Thames. I know not whether it had been founded by Alcott, Emerson's friend and neighbour at Concord, Massachusetts, or only established in admiration of his eccentricity. The ways of the society were very much out of the common; but one morning the young German went beyond them. He was found in the garden digging "*mit nodings on.*" The poor fellow was crazy, crazier than the community could stand. Carlyle took charge of the stranger in his own house until friends in Germany could have care of him. Many hard words may be forgiven for such a generously gentle act.

Only twice after my visit to ask for his signature had I the good fortune to see Carlyle. Once, not long afterwards, at a festival given to my friend William Bridges Adams by his workmen at his railway-carriage building works, the Fairfield works at Bow, when Carlyle and Mrs. Carlyle, Mazzini, Miss Hays (the first English translator of George Sand), Lady Duff Gordon, Dr. Stewart, Miss Jews-

bury, myself and others, were guests. Carlyle spoke
on the occasion. " Might they always understand
industry and service as something more than mere
marketable commodities, and might no fool or
coward or liar ever be among them ! " (I quote
from a report I gave to the *People's Journal*.) I had
not much talk with Carlyle ; but more with his wife,
with whom I was much pleased. I recollect her
speaking of her childhood, of the times when she
was made a scholar and would rather have had a
doll. Once later, when Emerson was in England
and lectured at Exeter Hall (a grand lecture on
" Home," of which I have lost sight), I came out
from the lecture with Carlyle and Adams, and
walked some way along the Strand with them.

My visit to Leigh Hunt was only the first of
many to that most delightful of old men. I got at
last to be treated almost as one of the family, spend-
ing freely my evenings with them when I would,
listening to Hunt's pleasantly wise talk, while Mrs.
Hunt (a stout, genial, motherly woman, of whom no
one could have supposed that in her young days
she was threatened with consumption) peeled wal-
nuts for me. How well I remember one evening
when I was privileged to dine with Hunt and Eliza
Flower and Fox, at Fox's house in Queen Square,
Westminster, — only the four of us, and the two
men talking of the Old Dramatists, to which we
other two were content to be listeners. I walked
from the Square with Hunt to his house in Ed-

wardes Square, Kensington, he finding something to say of every notable house on our way, and was taken in with him. Late as it was, he sat down to his beloved piano, playing among other things Purcell's "Halcyon Days," from the *King Arthur*. It was an evening never to be forgotten, of which I fain would have notes, to speak more fully.

CHAPTER VII

The Howitts; Tennyson; The Toynbees; Mazzini; Worcell; Stolzman; The Bandieras; Letter Opening at the Post Office; Carlisle
Election.

IT may have been some years later that I knew the
Howitts, when I knew them living at Upper Clapton, beyond Hackney. Howitt was a square, stur-
dily built, but not large, Quaker, who, when out,
generally carried a big stick: the type of the
Quaker who would not take up arms, but who, when
the ship on which he was a passenger was boarded
by an enemy, held out his hands against one of the
boarders with the quiet remark, "Friend! thee
hath no business here," and pushed him off. William Howitt's inoffensive stick might have come
into play under such warranty. I think he was
not a quarrelsome man, though quick-tempered, and
he could be angry at opposition. Mrs. Howitt was
the gentle, primitive Quakeress, a comely woman,
good, and very kindly. Her writings seem to reflect
her nature. It was a great pleasure to me, many
years after I supposed I must have passed out of
remembrance, to receive a most cordial letter from
her, then an aged woman living in Switzerland, in
answer to a request for leave to print in England
some of her poems. At the Howitts' house in

48

Upper Clapton I once breakfasted with Alfred Tennyson, not much impressed by his appearance, speech, or manner.

Friends of Wade were the two brothers Toynbee, George, a literary man who died young, and Joseph, afterwards eminent as an aurist, the father of Arthur Toynbee, whose memory is kept alive by " Toynbee Hall." George was one of the first acquaintances made in England by Mazzini, and to Mazzini I was introduced by Joseph. In 1841 Mazzini established at No. 5 Greville Street, Hatton Garden, a free school for the poor Italians in London, most of them the wretched organ-grinders and hawkers of plaster casts. Here Joseph Toynbee, with Mazzini himself, and a few of his Italian refugee friends, taught nightly, with lectures on Sunday evenings. Pistrucci, a remarkable improvisatore, brother of a clever medallist in the Mint, was director and also a teacher here. And here one night I met, at one of the school meetings, a little plain Yankee woman, Margaret Fuller, plain, but interesting and attractive, whose speech was earnest and to the purpose. I had some after correspondence with her from Italy.

Mazzini introduced me to two Polish friends, refugees and exiles like himself, Stanislas Worcell and Karl Stolzman. Worcell, a Count of Volhynia, had been the owner of large estates, which he forfeited on account of his prominent share in the Polish insurrection of 1830. He raised a troop on

E

his own lands, fought his way into Warsaw, and sat there in the Polish Senate. He was a man of middle height, of noble presence, and of most re-markable culture and intelligence, the chief of the Democratic party in the Polish Emigration, although nearly related to the royal Czartoryskis. In the course of years, with very much intercourse with him, I became as intimate with him as with Mazzini. I might say even more intimate. He was a man to revere and love, a saintly martyr, a true hero, a wise philosopher, and a man whose knowledge seemed to be unbounded. He was Mazzini's closest friend. Stolzman, a tall, stalwart man of military bearing, was an old soldier, who in his youth had served under Napoleon. Returning to Poland after the Imperial fall, he, as an artillery officer, did good service in the defence of Warsaw, for which, by General Bem, famous afterwards in the Hungarian War, he was promoted to the rank of colonel. Meeting with Mazzini in Switzerland, he aided in the formation of the Society of " Young Europe," founded by Mazzini to bring together the Republi-cans of the different countries.

In 1844, letters from abroad to Mazzini and Stolzman were opened at the English General Post-Office in London. Of course they were in correspondence with Italian and Polish patriots. Lord Aberdeen was then the English Foreign Secre-tary, and Sir James Graham was Home Secretary. Some unimportant letters from Lovett and myself to Mazzini were also opened. These various letters were not only opened, but were afterwards resealed and delivered as if they had not been meddled with. At this time two young Italians, officers in the Austro-Italian Navy, Attilio and Emilio Bandiera, the sons of a vice-admiral in the Austrian service, were planning an Italian insurrection, from which Mazzini was endeavouring to dissuade them as inopportune. Information, stolen in the English Post-Office, from their letters to him, was given by Lord Aberdeen to the Austrian ambassador, which information was made use of to decoy the Bandieras into a vain attempt on Calabria, where with seven companions they were stalked down, taken prisoners, and shot to death.

At first we were only aware of letters being delayed; and only by accident found out that they were opened and resealed (at that time it was still the custom to seal letters with wax). Then we learned the method : which was to take an impression of the seal, then carefully to break it, and afterwards, first slightly heating the surface of the wax, to press the counterfeit stamp precisely as it had been done before, so that there was no alteration of position, nor outward appearance of any kind to show that the seal had been tampered with. But they could not prevent the breakage of a hair or slip of paper placed under the seal as a means of detection; and the heating of the wax was only on the surface just enough to take the new impression, leaving the main underbody of the seal broken. This I discovered by happening to keep a letter loose in my pocket for a couple of days, when the surface-joined seal sundered and revealed the procedure. We also obtained exact information from a subordinate in the Post-Office.

Then I took the matter to Thomas Slingsby Duncombe, the radical member of Parliament for Finsbury, a man chivalrously prompt to notice any political grievance. At first he would not believe me, but when convinced, gave himself heartily to the exposure by bringing it before the House of Commons. After much official evasion and shuffling and opposition on the part of the government, Duncombe obtained from the Commons the appointment of a Select Committee of Inquiry (himself not named on it and the inquiry secret); and Lord Radnor obtained a similar committee from the House of Lords. The reports of the two committees (that of the Lords sitting later and so fuller) did not agree, each reporting only what they supposed to have been discovered by us. We knew more, but were not called to produce our evidence. On occasion of the debate in the Commons, Duncombe got the admission of Mazzini and myself to the floor of the House, and I heard Shiel (harsh-voiced but eloquent), Wakley, and Macaulay, in denunciation of the outrage. A full account of the parliamentary proceedings and of the whole affair is given by my friend, Dr. Lonsdale of Carlisle, in his life of Sir James Graham in the *Worthies of Cumberland*, published by Routledge in 1868. Public feeling for a time ran high. *Punch* caricatured Graham as Paul Pry at the Post-Office; Leech drew a pictorial parody of Mulready's design for the Post-Office envelopes, with Graham for principal figure in place of Britannia; letters were posted with "not to be Grahamed" on the outside; indignant public meetings were held; but after a while, as there was no personal interest involved, the excitement died out. But Graham's share in the business was not forgotten.

Some years after this, while living in the Lake Country at Brantwood, beside Coniston Water, I went to Carlisle to meet my friend Mr. Joseph Cowen from Newcastle; Carlisle a sort of half-way for each of us. We spent a night together, and separated next day. But it was the eve of an election, and Sir James Graham was a candidate, and we happened to visit the Working Men's Association; so it was immediately assumed that I could only be in Carlisle to annoy Sir James by reviving the old Post-Office scandal, there, perhaps, as a tool of the Tory party to oppose him. Surely I had no thought of being a candidate for parliamentary honour or of interfering with the election, but the disgrace of the *espionnage* had clung to him. After all, not Graham, who suffered most as cat's paw, but Aberdeen, who had passed on the stolen information to Austria, was the worse offender.

The story of the Bandieras, of their patriotism, their betrayal, and their fate, I heard from Mazzini's own lips, as he walked with me in the forest on one of his visits to me at Woodford.

CHAPTER VIII

Partnership with John Orrin Smith; Artists and Work; *Illustrated London News;* Ingram; *Punch;* Jerrold; Leech; the Doyles; Lady Morgan.

IN 1842 I became the partner of John Orrin Smith, a good and eminently successful engraver in wood, for whom I had worked for several years, and so, leaving Woodford, came to live again in London; first in Judd Street, Brunswick Square, and then at 85 Hatton-Garden, Holborn; after a little while taking my family back to Woodford, retaining 85 Hatton-Garden as my place of business. My connection with Smith brought me among the artists whose drawings, with the help of a dozen or so of pupils and journeymen, we engraved. Chief of these artists, still retaining the popularity he had gained almost immediately when, Bewick's favourite pupil, he came to London from Newcastle, was William Harvey, most prolific of draftsmen, most amiable of men. Him I had known before I joined with Smith. Through Smith I knew Kenny Meadows, then completing an *Illustrated Shakspere*, and also drawing the *Heads of the People*, a clever series of character heads for which the letter-press was written by Douglas Jerrold, Horne, Laman Blanchard,

Dickens, and others. The editor of the *Illustrated Shakspere* was Stanton the chess-player, a tall, handsome, genial man, whom I knew slightly. We also engraved John Gilbert's drawings for an edition of *Cowper*, the most careful and, I think, almost the best, although the earliest of Gilbert's numerous works. He had not then begun to draw for the *Illustrated London News*. For the *Bell's Life in London*, a weekly sporting newspaper, we engraved outline portraits of horses, the winners of the Ascot, Epsom, and Goodwood races, drawn by Herring, the animal painter; and other few illustrations — once a whole side of the paper, on occasion of the birth of the Prince of Wales. In the editor's room one day I had the honour of meeting a well-mannered, rather mild-looking man, over six feet in height, Mr. Winter, the landlord of a respectable public house in Holborn, who in his younger days had been known as Tom Spring, the champion pugilist of England. John Leech's first drawings were submitted to us, and found ready appreciation.

For the *Illustrated London News*, after its first year, Smith & Linton did a great amount of work, from drawings by Harvey, Meadows, Gilbert, Duncan, Dodgson, Leitch, and other artists; and copies of pictures by the old masters, and paintings in the annual exhibitions of the Royal Academy and the two Water-Colour Galleries. A very remarkable man was the proprietor of the *News*, Herbert Ingram, a Lincolnshire printer, who, having made some money by the sale of " Parr's Life Pills " (the recipe of Dr. Snaith of Boston), came to London and met with a projector named Marriott, from whom he obtained the idea of an illustrated paper. He found a good publisher, Joseph Clayton, the publisher of the *Spectator*, at that time the most important and best of weekly newspapers in London; and the *News* was soon a success. Ingram was a curious character: uneducated, without literary ability or knowledge or appreciation of Art (asking me once if I had leave from Guido to copy his " Aurora"), he seemed about the last man to be the conductor of an illustrated paper; but he had a kind of intuitive faculty of judging what would please the ordinary public, a perception of that which seemed never to fail. And he was enterprising and liberal. The paper was well edited, at first by John Timbs, who had been editor of the *Mirror*, a good book-worm and a man of much general information, and afterwards by Charles Mackay, the very popular poet. Stanton contributed the chess-column, and the management was promptly ready in engaging the best draftsmen on wood, in which Smith & Linton, and afterwards Linton alone, were able to be of considerable service. The paper had the good fortune to meet a public want, and also by its conduct deserved its great success.

Very different was the beginning of *Punch*, which was suggested by the *Figaro in London*, a smaller sheet, edited by Gilbert a-Becket and illustrated by

Seymour; for *Punch* started with a galaxy of talent, literary and artistic, since unequalled, — Douglas Jerrold, Mark Lemon, Thackeray, Henry Mayhew, Albert Smith, Leigh, (Hood came later), Leech, Tenniel, Richard Doyle, and Cruikshank. Most of these men I knew more or less. Jerrold I knew best, a little keen-faced man, bowed by rheumatism, the consequence of early privations. I have heard of him and a companion in early days, Laman Blanchard, afterwards known as a poet and wit, and, I think, editor of the *Court Journal*, sitting in their poverty and despair on a doorstep, meditating suicide. Once, coming from Herne Bay to London by steamboat, I saw Jerrold lifted on board in a chair, where, for the few hours' voyage, he sat movelessly, in pain, and fearful of anything coming near to touch him. Rheumatism, like gout, is not a good teacher of amiability; nevertheless I believe, for all the sometime cynicism of his sarcastic witticisms, that Jerrold was a kindly natured man, as melancholy Hood most certainly was. But even in the days of his late prosperity all was not smooth with Jerrold. He had many drags upon him. One, I fancied, was Henry Mayhew, a clever man about town, the author of *London Labour and the London Poor*, who married Jerrold's daughter, a girl not half his own age. Jerrold's wife's brother, Hammond, was lessee of the little Strand Theatre, at which Jerrold played the hero in his own charming little drama, *The Painter of Ghent*. I have spoken of Laman Blanchard. I only recollect his brilliant eyes and witty talk, once for a few hours in his company with Orrin Smith at the original Mulberry Club, before the club was made notable by Dickens. Albert Smith, the famous showman, began life as a dentist. I remember him when he was hoping for a practice in Percy Street, Tottenham Court Road. Tenniel was a tall, handsome, gentlemanly fellow, blind of one eye, which had been injured in fencing. Thackeray would sometimes drop in at 85 Hatton-Garden, and I came to know more of him and his kind-heartedness and generosities later. Leech, too, was tall, slight, and very handsome, and gentlemanly in his nature and deportment. His father had been proprietor of the " London," or " City of London" (I forget which of the two taverns and hotels), in Bishopsgate Street; and young Leech, when his artistic talent first appeared, was a medical student.

While I was living in Judd Street, I was one night roused from my bed by a policeman who came to say that a Mr. —— (I forget the name, but it was one I did not know) had been taken to the neighbouring police station and wished to see me. I went there and found Leech. It appeared that he and Leigh, going along the streets, perhaps returning from the weekly meeting of the contributors to *Punch*, had somehow jostled a stranger off the pavement, and there had been rough words and talk of assault, ending in Leech and Leigh being taken up. Leech was

sober, Leigh not.   So Leigh had to remain in " dur-
ance vile " while Leech returned with me, and we sat
up until his friend had recovered sufficiently to be
bailed out.   They had to appear in court next day,
and to suffer some small fine for the small offence.
" Like a leech? Sir!" remarked the police ser-
geant, recognising his man for all his assumed name
as he saw him drawing on his thumb-nail.   Leech's
marvellous talent in portrayal of character was a
natural gift.   He had no academical education, but
learned and grew by practice.   His drawing, except
his dainty little bits of landscape background, was
never good; but his hand never failed in rendering
vividly what his eyes saw.   Richard Doyle I do not
personally recollect; but I knew his eldest brother,
James, also an artist, though of less original talent.
There were three brothers, James, Henry, and Richard.   Once, at a conversazione given by the Institute
of Fine Arts at the " Thatched House " in St. James'
Street, I saw the elder Doyle, their father, the famous
caricaturist " H. B.," whose lithographs deserve to be
prized if only for the admirable portraits in them —
the very best portraits of men of the period.   At the
same conversazione I was introduced to Lady Morgan, a little wizened old woman.

CHAPTER IX

William and David Scott; Wells; Sibson.

WILLIAM BELL SCOTT I first knew in 1841. I may say at that date began our friendship, a friendship which happily lasted until his death in 1890. He was a son of Robert Scott of Edinburgh, an excellent landscape engraver in copper, after the delicate and expressive manner, and with much of the quality, of Milton, whose Irish and other views, but little known, are of the best engraving ever done. My friend, a year older than myself, was a tall, broadshouldered man, with a handsome face surmounted in young days by a fall of black hair (the whole of which he lost while yet in middle age), thoughtfully serious and rather reserved, but yet genial and attractive, throughout his early life looking older than his years. Poet and artist, he had come south in 1837 to seek his fortune; and in 1843 competed for the prize for the best cartoons, in the exhibition in Westminster Hall of the designs for pictures to be placed in the new Houses of Parliament. Though he obtained neither prize nor commission, and though his cartoon of the " Picts attacking the Roman Wall" was not so academically strong as some of the rival cartoons, it merited more consideration than most as a fine subject, well thought, well composed, and well drawn. It may, however, have led to his appointment as master of the School of Design at Newcastle-on-Tyne, in which capacity he continued, a very efficient and successful teacher, for many years, returning to London in 1864 on a pension for good service and as examiner of the drawings of the pupils at South Kensington.

A fertile designer, an excellent etcher and draftsman on wood, a good painter, an accomplished artist who, in his painting, only fell short of greatness, his most important work was a series of pictures on Northumbrian history on the walls of the hall of Sir Walter Trevelyan's house at Wallington. He also painted the story of the *King's Quair* (the poem written by King James the First of Scotland, during his imprisonment at Windsor) on the wall of a circular staircase at Penkill Castle, near Girvan in Ayrshire, some twenty miles from Ayr, the ancestral home of Spencer Boyd, with his sister, the last of a family not unknown in Scottish history. Among his etchings deserving of especial notice are those from his brother David's and his own designs for Bunyan's *Pilgrim's Progress*, published by the Fullartons of Edinburgh, and a series of selections from his brother's works published by the Art Union of Glasgow. His writings were many and of more than ordinary worth; a memoir of his brother David, the greater Scottish painter, accounts and criticisms of the " Little Masters," a *Life of Durer*, various other manuals on Art, and poems, one the *Year of the World*, a philosophical poem of which Emerson spoke to me admiringly. A handsome volume, published in 1875, with etchings by Alma Tadema and Scott himself, containing " Ballads, Studies from Nature, Sonnets," etc., ranks high, though neither popular nor well known, among the verse-work of the nineteenth century.

David Scott, an elder brother of William, I knew also, but not so intimately; visiting him in Edinburgh, and once visited by him on occasion of his being in London to see his brother. I was then living by the forest-side at Woodford. Two coaches ran between the city and Woodford. By the first, one Sunday morning, came David Scott to spend the day with me. By the second came an unexpected visitor, Charles Wells, in youth a friend of Keats, in emulation of whom he had written a quite-forgotten drama of *Joseph and his Brethren*. Two men differing more in outer appearance and in nature could hardly have been brought together, both men of mark. Scott, tall, severely handsome, but with a melancholy expression, the sadness of a high-soaring and disappointed artist; Wells, under the average height, spare and wiry, alert, looking as if he might be a fox-hunting sportsman; Scott, a poet, his art held by him as an apostleship; Wells, not more poetically enthusiastic in delivery than in appearance. For myself, I was at that time chiefly possessed by political fervour, in which neither of my visitors had any interest. How we three could pass an agreeable day together I now hardly imagine, yet I recall it as a notably pleasant time till my two guests departed together in the evening. This must have been in 1846.

I had become acquainted with Wells in 1845 through reprinting some of his *Stories after Nature*, a little book I had picked up at a book-stall in 1842, and which had charmed me with its originality and freshness. In 1845 I was editing the *Illustrated Family Journal*, a weekly *mélange* of Tales, Essays, and Verse, and in the latter half of the same year, I succeeded Douglas Jerrold as editor of the *Illuminated Magazine*, a monthly issue of the same character. In both these magazines I printed some of Wells' *Stories*. How he, then living in Brittany, got sight of the reprint, must, I think, have been through the younger Hazlitt, with whom he was in some way connected by marriage. He (Wells) wrote to me, thanking me for having used them, and sent me two other stories in manuscript. One, *Claribel*, I printed; the second I returned, and have ever since regretted that I did so. It was powerfully written, but too gruesome for a popular serial: the story of a man discovering his wife with her lover, shutting them up together to starve to death, and years afterwards opening the closed chamber to contemplate his revenge. So, as I have said, when in England he came to see me, and was very friendly, giving me a copy of the *Joseph and his*

Brethren, published, if unsuccessful bringing out can be called publishing, two years after the death of Keats, under the pseudonym of H. L. Howard.

Both of Wells' books I lent to Dante Rossetti, who much admired them and talked of illustrating the *Stories* for my engraving; the project, however, fell through. Except for the reprints of the few *Stories* in the two magazines, until the republication of *Joseph and his Brethren,* with a preface by Swinburne, in 1876, Wells remained unknown, only heard of by the mention of his name in 1877 in a scarcely noticed sonnet by Keats, — " To a friend who sent me some roses " ; his name again, followed by a line, " whose genius sleeps for its applause," and an admiring note to justify the line, in Wade's *Contention of Death and Love,* in 1837, and some later praiseful words by Rossetti in a supplementary chapter to Gilchrist's *Life of Blake.* So buried in neglect was the work of one who, in the words of so capable a critic as Swinburne, " will some day be acknowledged among the memorable men of the second great period in our poetry." A strange fight against oblivion has been the fate of Wells. I dare to claim some share in the endeavours at an honourable rescue. I lost sight of the man when, after a short stay in London, he returned to Brittany. The *Stories after Nature* were reprinted in 1891, by Messrs. Lawrence and Bullen, with a few prefatory words by myself.

David Scott I knew afterwards at his home in

F

Edinburgh, when, on a visit to my friends the Fullartons, the publishers, I found time to visit him and see his pictures in his own studio, too many of them there unsold and unprized; for he also, although the President of the Scottish Academy, had not in life the full meed of appreciation, little known indeed south of the Tweed. A great man every way was David Scott, one of three or four men who attracted Emerson when in England, and whom Emerson cared to recollect. One of his best works is a half-length portrait of Emerson, now in America, in the Public Library of Concord, Massachusetts. His great picture of "Vasco de Gama encountering the Spirit of the Cape" is in the Trinity House of Leith. Even now his multifarious work is chiefly known by his brother's loving *Memoir*, and by engravings from his pictures, great as his work was, the greatest of Scottish Art, great in the wide scope of his imaginative power and, to those who know his pictures, in masterful accomplishment. In the words of Margaret Fuller, one saw in him "a man, an artist, severe and antique in spirit; he seemed burdened by the sorrows of aspiration, yet very calm, as secure in the justice of Fate." He died in 1849. A memoir of considerable length in the *Art Journal* was printed, with my name to it; what I had written much cut down by the unscrupulous editor, Mr. S. C. Hall, apparently only because praise of the dead, even without direct comparison, might seem to detract from the merits of the living.

Hall, who sat to *Punch* for Pecksniff, a truer likeness than that which Dickens unfairly and unhandsomely attempted to fasten on Leigh Hunt, acted as unworthily as toward me with a notice which was sent to him by W. B. Scott of another artist to whom Scott and myself were much attached, and of whom we were proud, Thomas Sibson, a young man of great promise and some excellent performance, now utterly unknown. He was the younger son of a Cumberland farmer, an elder son, Francis, when I first knew him, being house-surgeon at Nottingham Hospital. Afterwards he was Physician to the Consumptive Hospital in London. Thomas had been placed with an uncle in a mercantile house at Manchester, but enthusiastic for Art, and surely feeling his own genius, he started moneyless and on foot to London to become an artist. There, I know not how, he dropped on Wornum, a young painter trying his hand ambitiously on big unnoticed pictures ; a man, however, of much culture, and in due time the Keeper of the National Gallery. He met also with W. B. Scott, who took frankly to him, and at whose house, Scott and I already close friends, I first saw him and became attached to him. A tall, spare, not handsome youth he was, looking like a sinewy countryman, yet soon showing symptoms of a consumptive tendency ; earnest, quick, and quaint and humorous, attractive and winning, and thorough in devotion to his art. His first work of importance was a series of etchings, designs in illustration of Dickens' *Old Curiosity Shop* and *Barnaby Rudge*, by a long way the best illustrations of Dickens' Works (I speak of them from present knowledge, corroborative of earlier perception), but the publication, a weekly issue without the text, was not successful pecuniarily. Then he began for me illustrations for a *History of England*, which my young ambition projected as a desirable work, in which the social life of the English people should be dominant, and its epochs so distinguished, instead of by the reigns of Kings. For this he made for my engraving many drawings of a size for an octavo page, admirably designed and drawn. Not satisfied with them, he cancelled them all, and resumed his work on a larger scale.

Every Thursday, the day of sending in my weekly engraving for the *Illustrated London News* (which gave me a half-holiday, after probably late sitting up the night before), he would come to meet me, and we would ramble together, with much talk of Art, through the Kentish Town fields (all built over now) to Hampstead Heath, dining at "Jack Straw's," the Heath hotel, and finishing the day with a pipe at Scott's house in Kentish Town. His genius was so apparent that, with the outfit provided by some friends, he betook himself to Germany to place himself as a pupil in Kaulbach's school. Arrived at Munich, he found that the school had been given up; but the master received him with kindness, examined his drawings, and with the generosity of one of the

Old Masters took him as a pupil free of all charge. With Kaulbach in Munich, working well, he remained for a year or more, returning to England only to find that as his art progressed his health was failing. He came to live with me, soon too weak for serious study. I used to bring him, when he became too feeble for continued walking, gatherings of wild flowers, rose, briony, folk's glove, and others, of which he would draw in pencil large masterly cartoons. Some of these, when I came to America, I gave to my friend Dr. Rimmer, at that time master of the free drawing school at the Cooper Institute in New York, thinking so to make them useful. They were admirably drawn. At last he had to cease from even such comparatively easy work, and the only chance for his life appeared to be a voyage to the Mediterranean. A ship was found for him; one sailing to Odessa from Newcastle-on-Tyne, and I accompanied him to Newcastle, staying, till the ship was ready, with friends of the captain at Blaydon House, then the residence of Mr. Carr, who had been mayor of Newcastle. We left Newcastle one evening, ominously scraping the Bar as we went down the Tyne, and next day had a rough passage, and on the following morning a fog, in which our ship struck on Filey Brig, an outlying reef of rocks some seven miles from Scarborough on the Yorkshire coast. We got safely on shore after a few hours, and two days later I took my poor friend by easy journeys to his brother at Notting-

ham. Some little while afterwards he was carried
to Malta, only to die there before many weeks had
passed. He gave promise of becoming a master
painter had he lived, and so industriously observant
was he that he left a collection of fourteen hundred
sketches, in a volume now in the Print Room of the
British Museum, beside the few designs for our
History, excellent both in conception and in execution; designs in my possession, I regret to say, yet
unpublished.

CHAPTER X

Bennoch & Twentyman; Haydon; Meadows; Henning; Other Artist Friends; Hall's *Book of Ballads; The National*, a Library for the People; Mutual Instruction Society; Chartist Meetings; Institute of the Fine Arts.

SIBSON's going to Malta was helped by the generosity of a friend, Mr. Richard Twentyman, of the firm of Bennoch & Twentyman, silk agents, and wholesale dealers in gimp, of Wood Street, Cheapside. Francis Bennoch was something of a minor Scottish poet, and Twentyman, by the loan of pictures to copy, was the helper and encourager of the youthful aspirations of Holman Hunt, whose father was in the employ of, I believe, a neighbour merchant in Wood Street. There was a story of Twentyman, soon after the beginning of Hunt's pictures obtaining notice, seeing the father, and being met, on inquiry as to the son's progress, with the naïve remark, "O, Mr. Twentyman! that pre-Raphaelitism is a grand invention." Bennoch and Twentyman were liberal men, and at their daily luncheon in the house, artists were specially welcome. There I met Haydon, some of whose smaller pictures belonged to Bennoch, one I well remember of the "Death-Cart, carrying victims to the place of execution" during the French Revolution,—only a sketch in oil, but finer than anything else I can recall of Haydon's. He was a sturdy-looking man, not a little self-assertive. I once heard him lecture eloquently on Art; and I take it that he was a better lecturer and critic than a painter, his pictures not wanting in force but exaggerated in form. We owe to him the first appreciation of the Phidian Marbles brought to England by Lord Elgin. Speaking of these, I am reminded of small copies of the frieze, with restoration of the mutilated parts, cut in slate, for casting in plaster, by John Henning, a Scottish sculptor of real genius. There was a long series of the Parthenon and Phygalian, some forty feet in all, about three inches in height, done with excellent accuracy, wonderfully strong and delicate. He gave me a set of them. He was a keen, energetic Scot, of average height, with a noble head. He died, I believe, aged over ninety, of cancer in his face. A son of the old man, John, had much of the father's genius, but turned it to no account. A second son, Archibald, was a fair and prolific draftsman on wood. A daughter was the wife of Kenny Meadows.

With Meadows I had much association, engraving many of his drawings for his *Shakspere* and the *Heads of the People*: a witty man, with some inventive talent, but a poor draftsman, having had little artistic education, brought up, one might say, on Finden's *Book of Beauty*, and the like wishy-washiness. I would often spend an evening at his house, or he would come to mine. There would be interchange of visits with Scott and Duncan. W. Leighton Leitch, the landscape painter (the "man with the itch," as Jerrold called him — he was a Scotchman — to distinguish him from John Leech), Dodgson, Topham, Franklin, were also of those who were my visitors and friends. Some I knew through their having to draw for me for the *Illustrated London News*; some, the great copper-engravers, John Pye, Lupton, Willmore, and Edward Finden, as fellow-members of the Artists' Annuity Fund; some, Young Mitchell (afterwards master of the Sheffield Art School), my close, dear friend Edward Wehnert (the water-colour painter), George Raphael Ward, the last of our great mezzotint engravers (the son of James Ward, R.A., disregarded as a poor painter in my young days, painting almost to the age of ninety, but after his death found to have been in his prime one of our greatest painters of landscape and animals), J. P. Knight (the genial Secretary of the Royal Academy), — these I knew as members of the Institute of Fine Arts, formed in 1846, at which, at our rooms in Great Marlborough Street, I used to join them at meetings of the council. Such connection with Art, added to my necessary business associations, made me more or less personally acquainted with artists. Among the principal not yet mentioned, I may name George Lance, the fruit-painter (only a fruit-painter, but of whom I have heard Haydon speak as one of the very few good figure draftsmen at that time in England, a man universally liked, whose quaint manner seemed of the Charles Lamb kind); John Gilbert, a pupil of Lance; Archer, Lance's brother-in-law, and Hine (two good archæologists); Tenniel; George Cruikshank; the younger Pickersgill; Richard Dadd (a talented and most amiable young painter, who went out of his mind, and in a paroxysm killed his father); Von Holst (an eccentric, clever German); McIan (a fierce Scotch Catholic); Fahey (the Secretary of the New Water-Colour Society); Henry Warren (the President of the same); Elmore, Frost, and Hart (Royal Academicians).

Many of these men, Scott, Sibson, Franklin, Meadows, Von Holst, Dadd, McIan, and perhaps others, engaged with Smith & Linton on Hall's *Book of British Ballads*, for some time attended the receptions given by Hall and his amiable and clever wife, Mrs. S. C. Hall, the Irish writer, at their house in Brompton, "the Rosery" (which some of us afterwards irreverently called the Roguery), where we were entertained with small talk and smaller Marsala, the flavour of which we, coming out together, generally corrected with a more pleasant potency at the nearest tavern. The *Book of Ballads* was an unfortunate investment, as the publication was not successful, and the failure left some of us unpaid. Smith & Linton lost largely.

The years of my London life, from 1838 to 1848, were busy years. In 1838 I was a reader in the old Reading Room at the British Museum, for several months a close student while preparing for the issue of a cheap weekly publication, which, as " *A Library for the People*," I hoped might supply the working classes with political and other information not open to them with their limited means for purchase and time for study, and scarcely to be printed under the laws then gagging the press. I asked Watson to publish for me, at my own expense. At first he tried to dissuade me from it, as likely to lead me into trouble personally as well as pecuniarily; but when he found me determined, he accepted and heartily helped. Six months exhausted my means. Settling with him, I noticed that he had not charged for folding the weekly sheets, or for folding and stitching a considerable number of monthly parts, the circulation having been much more than I had reason to expect, though not covering cost. No! he told me, he had been sure that I could only be a loser by the publication; and he and his wife "had done the whole of the work," a generous service not to be forgotten. In return I wrote for him a *Life of Paine*, which for a number of years had a continuous sale. About the same time I translated from the French Paine's *Address for the Abolition of Royalty*, its first appearance in English.

When I became a partner with Orrin Smith in 1842, I of course gave up the editorship of Hetherington's *Odd-Fellow;* but I was not asked to give up my interest in political matters, though often by one artist friend or another remonstrated with for the impolicy of my open association with chartists and the like. Indeed, by highly respectable and most pious folk Chartism was considered vulgar and disreputable. Certainly I lost friends, some good friends, dear to me, and whose friendship might have been valuable, by my independent action. After Smith's death in 1843, which left on my hands the charge of a large business and the support of two families, my own and his, I began to feel the untoward consequences. One man, a low church publisher, told me plainly that he could not avail himself of engraving, however well done, by a man of such principles. Living later at Woodford, I came daily to my place of business at 85 Hatton-Garden, London, by the Woodford coach, returning by the same conveyance. My companions outside the coach were city men, bankers, and the like, whose residences were on the forest side. It was very long before I had so much as a " Good-morning " from them. The only offence I gave my neighbours was that I opposed the church-rates, and was known to be a chartist (as such an advocate for admitting low people to the suffrage), and that I had helped to establish a " Mutual Instruction Society " among the workingmen of Walthamstow, a village separated from Woodford by a strip of the forest. It was for this Society that on one occasion I became a veritable stump-orator. The Society was originated at a meeting to hear two missionaries from the Chartist Convention sitting in London ; and in consequence of the political colour so given, when the next meeting, the first of the Society, was to be held, the few men gathered together found that they were not to be admitted anywhere. We therefore held our first meeting in an open part of the forest, and I had to speak from the stump of a felled tree. We afterwards obtained a place of meeting on protesting that we had no illegal intentions. I there gave my first lecture — *Against Death-punishment;* and for the sake of the funds of the Society, engaged in a three-nights' discussion with a pious temperance preacher, who did not compliment me.

In London I was continually a speaker at chartist meetings, and an active worker for the cause; writing and lecturing, without profit to myself, and, as before said, with some damage to my business. Conducting a large engraving establishment, sometimes as many as twenty journeymen and pupils in my employ, whose work I superintended and with whom I worked, my public political action as well as my position on the Council of the Institute of Fine Arts interfered with my time. I did what I could to make up for this by many nights remaining in town, working at my engraving after returning from the Institute or from a public meeting or lecture. I was much helped by the exceptionally good work done by my people and by profitable employment for the *Illustrated London News*. The *News* folk at last thought it might suit them better to have an engraving establishment exclusively for their own use; and, with that view, stopped employing me, one by one drew off my workmen, and so broke up my business. Partly in consequence of this, and partly for sake of the health of my family, my term of partnership with Orrin Smith and of responsibility to his family being ended, in the spring of 1849 I left London to reside at " Miteside," near Ravenglass, on the Cumberland coast.

CHAPTER XI

Ebenezer Jones; Our Visit to the Lake Country; A Tour in Scotland; London Life again; Prosecutions for Blasphemy; Haslam; Shelley; A Characteristic Incident; The Queen's Bench Prison; Powell; Roebuck; Thomas.

I HAD fallen in love with our beautiful mountain land in a hasty ramble through it two, it may have been three, years before with a poet friend, Ebenezer Jones, a clerk in a tea-dealer's house, who had ventured to indulge in dreams of poetic fame. A true poet he was, if not a great one, the author of a volume, *Studies of Sensation and Event*, published in 1843, very characteristic of the young man's impressionable nature, his impulsiveness and sense of beauty, but which utterly failed of public appreciation. I was much attached to him, and we had frequent companionship during years in London following 1841. Our Lake Country ramble, the first visit to that beautiful district, is also a thing to be remembered. Here I may repeat some few words from *Reminiscences* of my friend prefixed to a reprint of his poems in 1879.

I was writing of our journey to the Lakes, a week's holiday there from London work. " How well to this day I can retrace our steps and recall the pleasant, bright companionship, that, like the sparkle in wine, made that pleasure-draught but more enjoyable; our delight in the moonlight walk from the Windermere Station by the Lakeside to Ambleside, that loveliest five miles in all England; our next day's climb (the track missed) over the Stake Pass, after bathing under the fells in a pool at the head of Langdale; how we lingered, dallying with our joy, on the mountain tops till night came on, a cloudy night of late September, after a day of autumn glory, overtaking us before we could reach the Borrowdale road; how, unable even to grope our way, we lay down together on the stones to sleep, and awakened by rain, crept under an over-hanging rock, and cold and hungry, smoked our pipes and talked till the dawning light enabled us to find a path to Stonethwaite; how we sat in a cottage porch to await the rising of the inmates and welcome a breakfast of bad coffee and mutton-ham so salt that it scarified our mouths. No grave-minded man was either of the pair who went laughing and singing, if somewhat limping, on their way; nor was there much disposition to gravity two evenings later when, after supper, at the little Fish Inn at Buttermere, we amused ourselves with improvising verses (certainly never printed) not exactly in honour of

'William Marshall, William Marshall,
Cotton-Spinner of Leeds.'

Verses of mere rhythmical extravagance in proper poetic execration of the factory-owning plutocrat who had the impudence to possess the one grand house in pastoral Buttermere. Full capacity for enjoyment, whether of his senses or his intellectual faculties, characterised the man in his day of health : delighted with all he saw, from the rugged bleakness of Wastdale to the pastoral repose of Buttermere, enjoying equally a row on Crummoch Water and our evening walk beside the golden woods to Keswick. This was Ebenezer Jones, the City Clerk, not too much disappointed at a literary failure before his heart was saddened (by domestic infelicities) and his health destroyed." The man was of the type of Alcibiades, but with an idea of duty which the Greek had not, which made him heroic in a time of severe martyrdom ending only with his death from consumption, in 1860, aged forty years. Beside his poetry he wrote also a very vigorous pamphlet during the Irish famine time, on the *Land Monopoly*.

His week's holiday over, Jones returned to London, in order that a fellow-clerk in the same house might take his turn at recreation. This young man went with a friend into Scotland, and four or five days later, the two were found dead on a hillside, having, as Jones and I had earlier, lost their way and laid down to sleep in the cold air. On parting from Jones, I, too, went on to Scotland, having a week's tour mapped out for me by my friend Leitch, the landscape painter. I parted from Jones at Penrith, and took train thence to Glasgow,

G

and the following morning left the busy city, taking the steamer down the Clyde to Dumbarton, going thence by coach to Loch Lomond. Up the western side of the Lake to Glen Crow, a little way along the Glen, I came at eventide upon a rude shanty tenanted apparently by only two small children, a girl nine or ten years old, and a younger boy. Father had come in tired from the field, and was abed; mother had gone to fetch home the kye. There was a small neat off-room where I could sleep; and the little lassie boiled for me a trout, fresh caught from the beck, which with rye bread and whiskey made me a capital late dinner, or rather supper. After a good meal I went down to the byre to make acquaintance with the mother, a bonnie peasant woman busy with the beasts. Then the whiskey was potent, and I thought it best to retire to my " prophet's chamber," where I slept soundly till late next morning, getting up then with a decided preference for tea. After breakfast I had my twelve miles' walk through the Glen, and through a powerful Scotch mist, to an inn by the side of Loch Long, where I dried myself before the great kitchen fire and was glad of another whiskey and of a plate of hot kail-brose offered me from the servants' table, to the evident disgust of the incoming landlady at a gentleman so misbehaving. But an offer of hot kail-brose was not to be despised on a wet day, when the traveler had yet another twelve miles to walk round the head of Loch Long and the head of Loch Fyne before the day's tramp was over and he could rest in his landlord's dry clothes and enjoy Loch Fyne fresh herrings (the best of herrings known) and a little more of whiskey at Inverary.

Next day it did not rain, but was gloomy; fit weather for the Inverary woods and dark Loch Awe. From Loch Awe is one long glen, returning eastward to the head of Loch Lomond. Nearly through the glen, but I knew not how near, I came upon a rough-looking fellow sitting by the roadside. He got up as I was passing him and walked on by my side. I did not like his look, and still less liked his halting behind me every minute to kick a stone out of the road. Some miles on we met a couple of fellows as rough as himself. They had some words in Gaelic with my companion, and the three stepped on with me. I thought it prudent then to wish them good evening and to hasten on ahead, with considerable haste so soon as I turned a corner and was out of their sight; and I was not sorry when I reached an inn where I put up for the night. Next day I walked by the western side of Loch Lomond to opposite Inversnaid. I was wondering how to get there when I fell in with a gentlemanly middle-aged man sauntering on the road, who told me I must light a fire on the beach and the smoke would be answered by a boat from the opposite shore. He took me into a two-roomed cottage in which he lived, the sitting-room lined with books as if he was some retired collegian playing recluse for the nonce, gave me matches, and showed me where to make my signal. Some children there helped me to gather sticks and, the fire lighted, there was quickly a boat across the lake. From Inversnaid next morning I had two pleasant young tourists with me over the fell to the head of Loch Katrine and down its eastern side to Lochs Achray and Vennachar. From there it was good road traveling to Callander and Stirling. Thence I went to Edinburgh to David Scott.

I go back to earlier happenings during my London life. I find it impossible in these Recollections to keep to strict chronological order. In 1841, when the Government visited its political opponents, the leaders of the working classes, with indictments for "blasphemy" (the pretext on this occasion the mere sale, among other miscellaneous publications, of an intemperate book by one Haslam, *Letters to the Clergy*, so pushed into notoriety), Heywood, the first prosecuted, advised retaliation upon Government partisans, that goose and gander might be served with the same sauce; and Hetherington, also indicted, took up the fight in London by indicting simultaneously four metropolitan booksellers of most unimpeachable respectability for the same disreputable offence, inasmuch as they had "published or exposed for sale the blasphemous and seditious" works of one Percy Bysshe Shelley, containing notably his *Queen Mab*, for which already, indeed many years before, William Clark had incurred and suffered the vengeance of offended law. We knew, of course, that the Shelley volume (the first complete edition of his poems) would only be well advertised by the prosecution, we had no desire that it should be otherwise; but if social obloquy and punishment for a conviction for "blasphemy" were to be so used against political opponents, we deemed it politic that boomerang-like they should return to plague their employers. Conviction was sure: law like physic always obedient to precedent. Our purpose was to prevent the trial of Hetherington or to affect his sentence. The first object was defeated. Hetherington's trial was prompt, while one or other of the counter-indicted attempted to evade trial by buying off our indispensable witness to the sale of the books, a compositor in Hetherington's employ, a former apprentice. They also got their trials postponed, seeing Watson and myself in daily attendance at the Court, as if we were fully prepared.

An incident in connection with this prosecution may help to show what manner of men were these "seditious" ones, stigmatised as stirrers up of strife, as of old, it is said, were certain other men, not unlike them, in Athens and Ephesus and elsewhere. Hetherington had determined not to pay a fine; "they might take it out of his bones,"—not so courtly an expression, yet of the same spirit as brave Sir John Eliot's defiance to Charles I. This later martyr had also his possessions, a shop, and books, and presses, and other printing material, besides household stuff. Once before all his belongings had been swept away; he would be craftier now. A few days before the trial I was with him calling upon the London agent of an old good friend, Hugh Williams, a Caermarthen lawyer. The agent had instructions to give to Hetherington a sufficient sum to buy his property. It was given without so much as an acknowledgment. Then Hetherington passed the money into the hands of one of his shopmen, Thomas Powell, who thereupon bought the property duly valued by a sworn broker to legalise the sale; and Hetherington, returning his friend's loan, went penniless into Court to meet the worst that could be inflicted. He defended himself with much eloquence and moderation, in spite of a bitter and unfairly personal attack of the prosecutor, Attorney-General Campbell (Lord Campbell afterwards); was complimented by Denman, then Chief Justice, and sentenced to the lightest punishment on record (the lightness, it may be, motived by the still threatened trials to follow), six weeks in a debtors' prison, that of the Queen's Bench, without a fine. Visiting him there was my only acquaintance with the inside of a prison, which I did not always feel sure of escaping. It was a not uncomfortable prison, with capital tennis grounds.

When he came out, we were still looking for the missing witness. One day, walking together, Hetherington and Watson came upon him; and their moral influence was sufficient to outweigh the inducement which had first captured him. He came into Court, gave evidence; and Moxon, the publisher of the incriminated book, the first to be tried, was, notwithstanding the eloquent pleading of Talfourd, found guilty. There was no escaping the jaws of Precedent. It remained only for the prosecutors to call the convicted " blasphemer " up for judgment, which of course was never done, personal animosity or revenge (Hetherington now out of prison) being beside the question; nor was farther proceeding taken against the other indicted "blasphemers," Frazer, Richardson, and Saunders of the firm of Saunders & Otley. We had gained enough. Prosecutions for blasphemy were estopped. I think there has since been only one, with foolish wilfulness provoked for the sake of personal notoriety.

It need hardly be said that Powell handed back the property when Hetherington came out of prison. He, Powell, a Welshman (Hetherington, I think, was also Welsh), graduating in patriotism, had had his twelve months' gaol lessons, suffering for hasty words used in preventing an outbreak; such a man clearly more dangerous than a mere mob-inciter. After the failure of Chartism he was active in organising a colonisation-party to South America. That too failed. He died a few years later in Trinidad.

It was at this time I made personal acquaintance with John Arthur Roebuck, the member for Sheffield, unpopular because of his endorsement of the New Poor Law, a staunch radical still, a man of influence in Parliament as a powerful and uncompromising speaker. He had undertaken for Hetherington to move an arrest of judgment, so that there should be some prolongation of the defence, and more of public attention insured for it. Calling to confer with him about it, I found him disinclined to take a part. He judged that it would be impolitic, that it would be taken as an aggravation of the offence. Finding him of such an opinion, and deciding that anything like a speech in mitigation or as a plea for mercy would be far from our purpose, I took away his brief (the motion for arrest of judgment was to be on the next day) and placed it in the hands of a younger and less known barrister, Ralph Thomas, who spent the night in preparing his speech, and spoke well to the question. Of course all we desired was the prolongation and addition to the defence: a second defence, in fact.

CHAPTER XII

Hugh Williams; Rebecca and Her Daughters; With Sibson in Wales; Travel Risks; St. Ives; Boulogne; Miteside; Brantwood.

HUGH WILLIAMS, the Caermarthen lawyer, a man of large business till he lost favour by his defence of poor men, was some little while after these Shelley prosecutions the instigator and undiscovered leader of the "Rebecca Movement," the one successful uprising in England since the Great Rebellion. It seems that power was vested in the local magistracy, or arrogated by them, to impose tolls on the highroads, and not only on the highroads, but even on by-ways to their own personal advantage. So great a grievance had this become in Caermarthenshire that the farming people at last secretly organised themselves and, masked and otherwise disguised, mostly as women, passed at night through the county, smashing the toll-gates and sometimes destroying the houses of the toll-collectors. The band was known as "Rebecca and her daughters," some Scriptural warrant being found for the name. Soldiers were sent into the district; but their interference was rendered of no avail by the universal sympathy with the movement and the clannishness

89

of the Welsh peasantry. "Going to catch Becky?" would be tauntingly sung out by the boys at the soldiers setting forth to stop some threatened outrage, misled, the attack being always elsewhere. I learned from Powell of Williams being concerned, and going for a holiday, and asked by the *Illustrated London News* to look out for anything worth picturing in the paper, I went directly to Caermarthen to visit Williams, whom I had met in London and knew both as a good chartist and as a friend of Hetherington. I dined with him one evening, and he sent me off to Pontyberem, some seven miles away, where next day was to be a gathering in favour of universal suffrage, a step beyond the toll-gate movement, which Williams from the first had meant as a preparation for farther political action. The meeting was held on a hill, attended by some thousands, a local magistrate placed in the chair, the chair in a cart, and all proceeded quietly and fairly. Going thence to a little inn in the neighbouring village, where I suppose Williams met his associates, he procured a horse for me, and we rode together to Caermarthen, where the same night I sent off a report to the *Morning Chronicle*, at that time the one liberal daily paper in London. Walking out with Williams next day, he owned that the Rebecca movement, so far unobstructed, was at an end. A numerous body of police had been drafted into the district and, scattered everywhere to watch individuals, secret action could no longer be maintained. Up to that time the Welshmen, with their usual tenacious fidelity to each other under all circumstances, had baulked every endeavour to trace the persons concerned. The movement was successful: the tolls were not reimposed. Williams' sister was the wife of Richard Cobden. "That was our bad uncle," said one of Cobden's daughters to me, many years afterwards, when I told her of my acquaintance with him.

I have spoken of my ramble through the Lake Country with Ebenezer Jones. That was not my first mountain experience. My first was with Thomas Sibson, before he went to Germany, I think in 1842. Taking train one morning from London to Birmingham, we walked thence the fifteen miles to Wolverhampton, through the " Black Country," black enough with coal and coal smoke everywhere until night-fall, when the innumerable fires burst forth, making our walk to seem almost like a passage through Hell. We slept at Wolverhampton, went by rail next morning to Liverpool, and the following morning by steamboat, I think, to Rhyll, and on foot to Abergeley. Then we set off for a walk along the northern Welsh coast, past where Llandudno now is, then not even projected, and under the wild out-jutting rock of Penman Mawr on the road to Bangor. It was a bright sunny morning, numerous larks in the air singing in chorus with the bass of the waves coming up the shore beneath them. Some way far on our road it came on to rain, and we found shelter in a toll-house. There sat a woman, the noblest form I ever saw, the living Milo Venus, or at least a Roman empress, paring turnips. I know we outstayed the necessity of the shower in admiring contemplation of the pseudo-empress; and ended our day's march, so shortened, at Aber, some miles short of our proper intention at Bangor. To Bangor next day and to the Menai Suspension Bridge, the wonder of the time, across the Straits to the Isle of Anglesea. Under the Bridge we bathed, then went on it; then returned through Bangor, taking, as we supposed, the road to Llanberris. Late in the afternoon we learned that there was a stiff bit of mountain range between us and our destination. This we ventured to cross, having our pathless direction by compass. After severe climbing, severer because it was our first experience, we reached the top only as darkness came on, so dark before we began to descend the other side that we could not see each other. We did not dare to stay on the top, so had to try the descent, letting ourselves slide, where it was too steep to walk, and guiding ourselves by the sound of many little waterfalls, which of course we avoided. At last we reached the bottom, found ourselves against a stone wall, and following it caught a perception of a white horse, and presently stumbled up against a cottage. To our knocking the door was opened by a young girl holding a light, with her black hair hanging below her waist. She started back, and an older man, we supposed her father, appeared, seemed to recognise us as belated travellers, and civilly piloted us into the road and to our inn. We were so tired that we were glad to lean on him, one on either side. Fortunately we had kept our right direction, and so were within a few hundred yards of the one little inn of Llanberris Pass, the "Vryneck Arms," where after a reviving dose of whiskey, we had our sodden boots pulled off, and hastened to bed, sitting up in bed to finish the day with ham and eggs, and probably more whiskey.

The next day, both of us suffering, Sibson from rheumatism, I from stiffness, we had to rest, only shambling a little way to Llanberris Lake. Another day, and we took the road through the Pass, the wildest and ruggedest in the country, so ruggedly precipitous we would not have ventured up in daylight where we came down in the darkness; and made, if I mistake not, a three days' journey, by Corwen, and Bettws-y-coed (for its beauty for many years a favourite resort of artists), and the Vale of Llangollen, to Shrewsbury. There we parted, Sibson going across the country to his brother at Nottingham, and I making for Monmouth, within a few miles of which I hoped to find the house of the young friend whom I had taken care of during Frost's trial, to whom I had promised a visit. A few miles out of Shrewsbury I fell lame (most likely I had strained myself on the mountain), and, instead of walking as I had intended, was glad of the coach to Hereford, and again next morning to Monmouth, landing there at breakfast time with, after feeing the coachman, a shilling in my pocket. Some previous experience had taught me to go to the best hotel. So I walked boldly into the "Monmouth Arms," and said I wanted a gig to carry me to Blackwood. Well, Blackwood was more than a few — it was forty miles from Monmouth. They could take me to Pontypool, where there would be no difficulty in getting farther conveyance. Indeed there would. "I have no money, so unless you can send me all the way I can not even have breakfast." Though how I, still a little lame, was to walk forty miles with only a shilling for food, I did not exactly see. A very little hesitation, and (I suppose they were not unaccustomed to the dilemmas of tourists) they would take me all the way. I had a splendid breakfast; the charge for that and the fee to waiter, for the gig and driver, and even the toll-gates, set down in my bill (and they did not overcharge me); and I went on my forty miles' ride on a bright summer day through one of the loveliest counties in England, reaching my friend's house in time for an early dinner, taken out of pawn, and welcomed. I stayed some days with him, returning to London by way of Bristol.

I had a careless habit, perhaps excusable in an artist, of going to the very end of my tether on such excursions. One Sunday evening I found myself at St. Ives, on the far end of the northern coast of

Cornwall, a great place for the pilchard fishery. But though after paying my inn-bill next morning my purse held but five shillings, I knew the date of a steamer from Bristol and was not afraid. As it happened, so making me sure, the sea was rough enough to prevent the ship from coming in, and passengers went to her in boats. The steward only came round for fares after the boats had left. At Bristol I gave my watch as security while I went ashore for money, having been this time wise enough to leave money there as I went on my round: a round to Exeter, Torquay, Plymouth, Falmouth, St. Ives, and back. At Exeter I had the fortune to arrive on an evening when the Devon Madrigal Society was dining there, and took up my quarters at the same hotel. Of good vocal music I have heard much, but nothing ever pleased me like the old English madrigals. Once on a visit to London I stayed some weeks at the house of a lady who before her marriage was known as Miss Thornton, the best of ballad singers. Her husband was musical, a friend living with them a musician also, and a fourth friend came in almost every evening to join them in madrigal singing.

To return to my travel-risks. One was on returning from Paris by diligence to Boulogne. The diligence should have reached Boulogne in time for the English steamboat, but did not get in till the boat had gone. It was noon, and I had to wait till next morning, with but little more money than would carry me through to London. The surplus was just enough to pay for a night's lodging, and only a few *sous* beyond for not much bread and some pears, on which I had to subsist till I got to London next day, going breakfastless from Boulogne to London. The previous afternoon I could only ramble about Boulogne. How I hated the place, not interesting under the best of circumstances.

Yet another time, this time deceived by distance, I had a similar fortune. I had come from London to Miteside to arrange for some repairs to the house I was about to live in. The distance from there to Kendal, where I would get the train to London, I understood to be about twenty-five miles. It was late when I left the house, and I had only covered some fifteen miles over the fells to Broughton by dark. I went into the little inn, had bread and cheese and beer, and asked for a bed. Having no luggage, they looked askance at me, possibly took me for a tramp, and were not inclined to harbour me. Only by my persistence, and showing determination to remain, they were at last overcome. I learned that I had still a twenty-five-mile walk across the fells to Kendal, and had to start before daylight. It was in February. A little way out of the town I found my feet sore; in fact, the skin was off my toes of both feet. And it was a cold and stormy day, wind and rain, and sometimes snow upon the ground, and the way rough and often steep. Again I had but a shilling beyond my railway fare: it gave me bread and cheese, once stopping to rest, and a glass of whiskey at a second halting-place. I appreciated in that day's journey what a sore-footed beggar, weary and wet through, might suffer. But I reached Kendal in time for the South train, and was in London next morning, very thankful to a fellow-passenger who gave me a sup of whiskey to keep out the cold. It was more than a few days before I had any pleasure in walking again.

At "Miteside" (the river Mite, a little stream coming out from the back of the Wast-water Screes) I lived for three years, barring occasional visits to London, until my landlord wanted the house for himself, when I found a home at Brantwood on the eastern side of Coniston Water, some nine or ten miles from Ambleside, a house under Furness Fells, in Monk Coniston, so called because the land had been part of the domain of the Cistercian Monks of Furness Abbey (Church Coniston village was on the western side of the lake). The manorial right had fallen to the Buccleughs at the time of the dissolution of the Monasteries; and to the Duke of Buccleugh, my portion of the land being copyhold, I paid a yearly fine of one shilling and three half-pence, to have my title recorded in the manorial books when after a year's tenancy I was enabled by the help of mortgage-money to buy the estate, — a fairly large house and ten acres of copse-wood steeply rising up the fell. I sold it to Ruskin years afterwards when I found I was likely to remain in America.

H

CHAPTER XIII

The People's International League; The Three Days of February; Congratulatory Address to France; With Mazzini in Paris; George Sand; Lamennais; *The Cause of the People*.

IN London, in 1847, at the instigation of Mazzini, and informed by him, the " Peoples' International League " was founded, with the following objects : —

" To enlighten the British public as to the political condition and relations of foreign countries ;

" To disseminate the principles of national freedom and progress ;

" To embody and manifest an efficient public opinion in favour of the right of every people to self-government and the maintenance of their own nationality ;

" To promote a good understanding between the peoples of all countries."

How necessary such an association was simply as a means of public enlightenment may be understood when even the *Spectator*, the highest priced and most thoughtful newspaper at that time in England, a paper which had as contributors such men as Carlyle, Stuart Mill, Bridges Adams, and Colonel Thompson, depended altogether for foreign information on the *Journal des Debats*, whose columns were closed to all popular movements in Europe. Mazzini's views in projecting the League may be given in his own words (not without interest even at the present time) in the address, which (with the exception of a wordy and unnecessary introduction by Mr. Philip Harwood) was from the draft prepared by him, a draft in his own handwriting, which I copied.

He wrote : —

"In the division of Europe among the several powers at the Congress of Vienna an immense error, not to say a great iniquity, was committed. The natural peculiarities of character, the indications of different destinies, the diverse natural tendencies of various peoples (deducible from their languages, creeds, habits, historical traditions, and geographical positions) were altogether overlooked or disregarded. Questions of the balance of power, of imaginary equalities, calculated by ciphers representing square miles or millions of men, not human ideas, human wants, human tendencies, were the considerations that decided the partition of Europe. It was a hurried, an ill-advised, and improvident work, concocted on the one hand by Powers that had nothing in view but their own despotic interests and aggrandisement, on the other by politicians looking no farther than their own time, seeking only for present peace, frightened at and weary of the convulsions through which Europe had just passed, and without faith in the future, — men anxious merely to reconstitute the old system which Napoleon had broken down, and who had given neither time nor sympathy to the study of those vital elements out of which a new system might be constructed, and upon which alone permanent peace and progression can be established. . . . The question now at issue throughout Europe, at the bottom of all European movements, is the question of nationality, of national rights and duties."

The League was initiated at a public meeting held on Wednesday, April 28, 1847, at the " Crown and Anchor " tavern in the Strand (the usual place for such meetings), Dr. Bowring, M.P., in the chair. The Council appointed at the meeting for the ensuing year were:—

Mr. W. Bridges Adams.
— W. H. Ashurst.
— Goodwin Barmby.
Dr. Bowring, M.P.
Mr. William Carpenter.
— Thomas Cooper.
— William Cumming.
— T. S. Duncombe, M.P.
Dr. Epps.
Mr. W. J. Fox.
— S. M. Hawkes.
— Thornton Hunt.
Mr. Douglas Jerrold.
— W. J. Linton.
— Richard Moore.
— T. Humphreys Parry.
— William Shaen.
— James Stansfeld.
— P. A. Taylor.
— P. A. Taylor, Jun.
— Richard Taylor.
— Joseph Toynbee.
— Henry Vincent.
— James Watson.

Messrs. Ashurst, Hawkes, Parry, Shaen, and Stansfeld were all young lawyers professing sympathy with the chartist movement, some of them practising public speaking at chartist meetings,— Parry, Stansfeld, and P. A. Taylor, Jun., being afterwards in Parliament; Richard Taylor was a Common Councillor of London, one of the old-fashioned school of educated printers, a man who edited a reprint of Horne Tooke's *Diversions of Purley*; Carpenter, a literary man, had preceded Hetherington in endeavours to break through the laws against the Press. Of other members I speak elsewhere. I acted as Honorary Secretary, and at my house, 85 Hatton-Garden, was the office of the Association, where the meetings of the Council were held. Usually these meetings were also attended by Mazzini, who would wait afterwards for a friendly talk with me over a glass of rum and water : rum, the one liquor from our West Indian possessions peculiar to England, and prized for its strangeness, as it seems to me, by all foreigners.

On the 15th of November, 1847, the League reported proceedings to that date to a public meeting of nearly fifteen hundred persons, held at the "Crown and Anchor," to give farther publicity to the views and intentions for the advancement of the objects of the Association. Dr. Bowring, M.P., was in the chair. The speakers were Colonel Thompson, M.P., Mr. P. A. Taylor, Jun., Mr. George Thompson, M.P. (the Abolitionist orator), and Mr. Linton.

The Report of Proceedings showed that the Address of the League (with a circular requesting coöperation) had been sent to the Members of both Houses of Parliament, to the entire Press of Great Britain and Ireland, to a large number of public institutions, political and literary, and to several thousand individuals, including many foreigners resident in England. It was favourably noticed and occasionally reprinted by a number of the British and of the Continental Press: among the latter, — in France, the *National*, the *Réforme*, and the *Démocratie Pacifique*, besides provincial journals ; in Belgium, the *Brussels German Gazette ;* in Germany, the *Bremer Gazette*, the *Frankfort Journal*, the *Berlin Gazette*, the *Upper Rhenish Gazette ;*

in Italy, the *Alba* of Florence ; in Switzerland, the *Helvetie* of Berne, the *National Gazette* of Basle, the *Nouvelliste Vaudois*, the *Narrator* of St. Gall, the *Review* of Geneva.   Many of these journals gave repeated notices.

The address had been translated into French, Spanish, German, Italian, and Polish.   Other manifestations of strong sympathy came from many parts of the Continent ; and in Switzerland the formation of the League was celebrated by public demonstrations in Berne, Lausanne, Basle, and Geneva ; and responded to by resolutions of several Swiss associations to support and join.

The Council had also published a pamphlet, written by Mazzini, on the question of the " Sonderbund " (the attempt to separate the Catholic Cantons from the Confederation) then agitating Switzerland.   This had been distributed among the four hundred members of the League, the Press, the Members of the House of Commons, and a number of public institutions.   It had been translated into French and German, and its statements approved by most of the Swiss journals.   Beyond this the Council of the League had been active in establishing communications with the principal cities of the Continent for the purpose of obtaining correct and ready information on all important questions.   Seventeen lectures also had been delivered in London upon the political condition of Italy and Switzerland, by Mr. R. H. Horne, Mr. Thomas Cooper, and Mr. W. J. Linton.

So much good work was accomplished by the League, and the work continued until the revolutionary events in Europe beginning with the February days in Paris, and the departure of Mazzini (the informing spirit of the League) for Italy, stayed proceedings; some of the Council seeming to think farther action unnecessary, others becoming indifferent. The last action was a congratulatory address to the Provisional Government of France.

The revolution in France in February, 1848, called forth the hearty sympathy of the working classes in England, of the chartists especially, they seeing in it a prospect of reinvigorating the chartist movement, which during some years had degenerated into a mere succession of desultory and purposeless speechifying. At a meeting called within a few hours of receiving the news of the Paris victory, Mr. J. D. Collett (the active secretary of the Association for the Abolition of the Taxes on Knowledge) and myself were deputed to carry the first address of congratulation, from working men in London, to the Provisional Government. We traveled to Paris in company with Mazzini; and, Collett returning almost immediately to England, I remained for more than a week, sharing lodgings with Mazzini. While there I had the opportunity through his introduction of an interview with "George Sand," a handsome matronly woman, from whom afterwards I had authorisation to translate her works,—a project which circumstances prevented my carrying out.

Through Mazzini also I came to know the venerable Abbé Lamennais, whom I had admired in younger days as the author of *Les Paroles d'un Croyant*. He had already begun a daily paper, *Le Peuple Constituant*, to teach the true principles of republicanism and, if possible, to help in guiding the course of public conduct in accordance therewith. Had his advice been taken, Lamartine's non-intervention manifesto had not betrayed the republican hopes of Poland, Italy, and the rest of Europe, and the terrible insurrection of June, of the Parisian working class, cheated by promises of vague and impracticable socialist theories, might have been avoided. I had a cordial reception from the old Abbé (he knew me by my translation, years before, of his *Modern Slavery — L'Esclavage Moderne*), a small, spare, worn man, physically weak, and poorly circumstanced, who was editing his paper in the one bare room in which he lived in the Rue Jacob; in spite of age and weakness fervent and energetic, a man truly of the stuff of which heroes and saints were made, if ever there was one. On one evening I went to see him he was out, and I waited for his return, on the stairs, talking with a lad who served him in circulating the paper. It needed not many words to tell me how this man whom the Pope feared and anathematised (" We damn forever this book of small size but huge depravity " — such the papal interdict on his *Words of a Believer*) could, nevertheless, be reverenced and loved. He gave me his paper, and

continued to send it to me in London until its sup-
pression by General Cavaignac on occasion of the
insurrection in June : Lamennais' sympathies, if not
approving their action, being with the Insurgents.
True to the people, when he died the little he had to
leave was left to none who had taken part against
them in those unhappy days.

Very strange at that time was the appearance of
Paris; the barricades not all cleared away; before
public buildings cannon, watched by lads of the
Garde Mobile ; the ante-rooms of the *Hotel de Ville,*
where the Provisional Government held its sittings,
guarded by men in blouses, the place having the
aspect of a mediæval incomplete revolt ; and strange
and strangely impressive the funeral procession of
those who had fallen in the Three Days, as from the
balcony of the *Café du Grand Balcon* I saw it
defiling along the Boulevard through the crowding
masses of Parisians, the Provisional Government on
foot as chief mourners, the roadway kept, not by
soldiers or police, but by a single tri-colour ribbon ;
every regimental or other band taking part, one
playing the " *Marseillaise* " and the next the song of
the luckless Girondins — " *Mourir pour la patrie,*"
even in that day of solemn triumph sounding like an
ill omen. For already it was plain that French
policy was separated from the nascent republican
hopes of revolutionary Europe.

Returning from Paris, with hope of reviving our
chartist agitation, I began the publishing of the

Cause of the People, a weekly newspaper, nominally edited by myself and G. J. Holyoake, but for which Holyoake did nothing.   At that date the Isle of Man, as well as the Channel Islands (Guernsey, Jersey, Alderney, and Sark), was exempt from duties imposed on the mainland; and taking advantage of this exemption, newspapers, which in all the country else passed through the post for a certain number of days free in virtue of the penny stamp upon them, passed freely without a stamp from these islands. So I had my paper printed and published in Douglas, in the Isle of Man, sending there the copy for the eight pages, and having the bulk of the printed matter sent through the post to my publisher in London (Watson), the single papers to be by him reposted free.   My venture lasted but nine weeks. After that, it may be to prevent a wider use of the precedent, the exceptional privileges of the islands I have named were withdrawn.   Duties also, on brandy, tobacco, etc., from which they had been exempt, were, I think, now imposed on them as upon the rest of the community.

CHAPTER XIV

A Day with the Irish; Writing in the *Nation*; Charles Gavan Duffy; *Conversations with Carlyle*; Carlyle and Duffy on Linton; Misrepresentations of Mazzini; Carlyle's Worth.

REFERRING to Sir Charles Gavan Duffy's *Conversations with Carlyle*, 1892, it seems that it was in 1845 he (Duffy), a young Irish friend named Pigott, and another Irishman, paid a visit to Carlyle. It is likely, therefore, that it was in that year (though I had thought it was not so early) that I made personal acquaintance with Duffy, breakfasting by invitation with him and Meagher ("Thomas Meagher of the Sword") at their hotel in the Haymarket. If this date be correct, I had already written for the Irish patriotic paper, the *Nation*. Mrs. Carlyle's description of Duffy, by him reported, is amusing. "With the coarsest of human faces, decidedly as like a horse's as a man's, he is one of the people I should get to think beautiful, there is so much of the power both of intellect and passion in his physiognomy." I agree with the intellect and passion, saying rather earnestness, but not with the coarseness or horse-likeness. My own impression was of a good-looking if not handsome, capable and honest man, to whom I was attracted as one fit to be a leader of men, and one whom I could trust. In Meagher, a taller and more personable man, I was not so much interested. He struck me as a self-assured, clever but rather raw collegian. He was in a fume at not having had his letters delivered to him, some of them having lain in the hotel office, his Celtic pronunciation of his own name differing from the English sound of *Meagher*, which even Landor used as rhyming with *eager*. I recollect that after breakfast I went with them to call on the young Pigott, whom Mrs. Carlyle also describes: " a handsome youth," she says, " of the romantic cast, pale-faced, with dark eyes and hair, and an 'Emancipation of the Species' melancholy," of whom she was disposed to predict that in case of an insurrection in Ireland he would " rise to be a Robespierre of some sort," sure some day to be beheaded. I should rather have likened him to the enthusiast St. Just. I never knew of him after that day till I saw mention of him in the *Conversations* of having become a successful advocate at the Indian Bar. With the four of us that evening dined Wm. Smith O'Brien, a tall, courtly gentleman of most prepossessing appearance and manner, a man, as shown in all his conduct, sincere to devotedness, chivalrous to very quixotism.

Some while after this I was to have met Duffy in London, wishful to confer with him in order to obtain some friendly coöperation of the Young Ireland party, with the remnant of the chartists, and with such " moderate reformers" as might be available; he was prevented from coming over from Ireland at the time appointed, and another opportunity did not occur. From the time I met him, as here related, I wrote in the *Nation* much verse over the pseudonym of "Spartacus" (the name I had used from my first writing in Hetherington's *Odd Fellow*), and over my own name occasional prose, chiefly on points in which I differed from the Irish party; specially (not so differing, I think) in 1847, in advocacy of "the right of the Irish people to the whole land of Ireland," and proposing the imposition of a tax of so much an acre, superseding all other taxation, for the prevention of another famine. In this I antedated the writing of Mr. Henry George.

When Duffy came out of prison in 1849, he asked me to join on the staff of the *Nation*. I refused only because I wished to remain a free lance. It was well. He had, when talking with me in England, demurred to my association with Mazzini, whose anti-papal course was not acceptable to the *Nation*, and who became the object of personal attacks which I could not but resent. I replied to them very bitterly, not more bitterly, I think even now, than they deserved, but with perhaps unneeded acrimony, too much for me to remain as a contributor to the paper. So we were sundered. Only four or five years ago came a letter to me from Nice, where Sir Charles Gavan Duffy was residing, couched in friendliest terms, ignoring all the offence which surely he had been warranted in keeping up.

It was a generosity which revived all the regard of old time, and renewed my respect for the character of the man.

Carlyle in 1849 had written to Duffy, among other bits of advice: "Also do not much mind Linton, who is a well-enough meaning but, I fear, extremely windy creature, of the Louis Blanc, George Sand, etc., species." On this Duffy comments as follows, and I am proud both of the higher appreciation and of the more than kindly feeling which prompted his remarks.

"Carlyle never saw Mr. Linton" [at that time he had twice seen me] "and misunderstood him, I think. W. J. Linton, the well-known wood-engraver (and who, judging him by the illustrations of one of his own poems, was also an artist of profuse fancy and skilful pencil), was less a French republican of the school of George Sand and Louis Blanc, than an English republican of the school of Milton and Cromwell, to which Carlyle himself may be said to have belonged. Like many gifted young Englishmen of the time, he found himself drawn toward the *Nation*, and contributed to it largely in prose and verse. The prose was, for the most part, controversial, justifying or illustrating opinions on which he differed with the editor; the poetry was incitements toward a generous and lofty nationality. I was delighted at the time, and still recall with pleasure the pictures he drew of the future we aimed to create." (*Conversations with Carlyle*, pp. 132–3.)

Before laying aside Sir Charles' book, I may note, there chronicled, some other hasty and misleading judgments of both Carlyle and his wife. " I asked him " (writes Duffy) " about the party of Young Italy and its leader. Mazzini, he said, ' was a diminutive, dark-visaged little fellow with bright black eyes.' Not dark-visaged for an Italian; and 'diminutive' hardly describes a man certainly not less than five feet and seven inches in height. But he may have been looked down upon by the tall Scotchman."

Carlyle went on to say: "Mazzini was a perfectly honourable and true man, but possessed by wild and fanciful theories borrowed from the French Republicans. He believed in George Sand and *that sort of cattle,* and was altogether unacquainted with the true relation of things in this world. The best thing that had ever befallen him was the opening of his letters by Sir James Graham; he was little known in London before that transaction; known in fact to few people except the circle in Cheyné Row. But afterwards he had innumerable dinner invitations, and got subscriptions up and down London for his Italian schools and other undertakings.

" (*Diary,* 1854.) I spoke to Mrs. Carlyle of Mazzini, whose name just then was a good deal in the papers. She said his character, which was generous and self-devoted, was greatly spoiled by a spirit of intrigue. He was always thinking what advantage he could get out of every occurrence.

" 'Advantage for his cause?' I queried.

" Yes! advantage for his cause, she said; but by methods such a man should scorn. It was he who planned the dinner of revolutionists at the American Consul's lately, which got the American Ambassador into such a scrape. The Consul, a young American — Saunders was probably his name — pestered Mazzini to dine with him. He would only consent on condition that Garibaldi, Kossuth, Ledru Rollin, and the rest were invited. An old Pole, it was said, had to borrow a sovereign to get his uniform out of pawn. Mazzini expected great results in Italy and Hungary from the false interpretation which would be put on this dinner with an American official. . . . In fact it was all a stage play, which Mazzini expected to produce the effect of a sincere and serious transaction.

"I said I had supposed him too grave and proud for anything like a trick. She said he was certainly grave and dignified, but he sometimes uttered trivial sentimentalities with this air of gravity and dignity in a way that was intensely comic. He was entirely engrossed in his purpose, however, while one of his brother triumvirs, a successor of Rienzi in the government of Rome, actually wrote to London to say that the *Westminster Review* need not despair of an article he had promised, he would send it with the delay of a month or two. This was a national tribune *pour rire*." (*Conversations*, pp. 109–11.)

I note so much (no doubt fairly reported by Duffy), not by any means wishing to attack the Carlyles, but in justice to Mazzini, here seen in an altogether false light through their prejudiced eyes. "That sort of cattle" may mark the value of the judgment of the fanciful historian, or rather dramatist, of the French Revolution. Mazzini did justice to the noble and high purpose of George Sand's writings, believed in her genius and the nobility of her nature; but he did not share her political theories nor in any way borrowed from French Republicanism. "A perfectly honourable and true man," "innumerable dinner invitations" and the getting of subscriptions for his Italian cause (the "other undertakings") might be no disparagement, though certainly he was far less a diner out than Carlyle himself.

Carlyle would have given to Duffy a truer impression of Mazzini had he but referred him to Carlyle's Letter to the *Times* in 1844, a letter containing the following: —

"I have had the honour to know M. Mazzini for a series of years, and whatever I may think of his practical insight and skill in worldly affairs, I can, with great freedom, testify to all men that he, if I have ever seen one such, is a man of genius and virtue, a man of sterling veracity, humanity, and nobleness of mind, one of those rare men, numerable, unfortunately, but as units in this world, who are called to be martyr souls; who in silence, piously in their daily life, understand and practise what is meant by that."

This is the real Mazzini, as Carlyle then knew him, and the character but little accords with that of one "greatly spoiled by a spirit of intrigue," "using methods a man should scorn," "planning a stage play" to produce a false impression, and uttering "trivial sentimentalities in a way that was intensely comic." But the worth of Mrs. Carlyle's judgment may be estimated by the uncalled for sneer at the Pole who "had to borrow a sovereign to get his uniform out of pawn" (there was no such Pole at the dinner), and the sneer at one of Mazzini's "brother triumvirs" (which could only mean Saffi), for writing to the *Westminster Review* concerning the delay of a promised article. Saffi was closely with Mazzini during that heroic defence of Rome, and certainly was not "a tribune *pour rire*." He was so well esteemed in England that when exiled he was given a professorship at Oxford, where probably he wrote to and for the *Westminster Review*. The dinner at the American Consul's was not "planned by Mazzini." Only he refused to accept it merely as a personal compliment, as other than a mark of American sympathy with the European Republicans, little knowing how scant such sympathy was, how bound was the generous "Republic" to the selfish and cowardly policy of not entangling itself with dutiful alliances.

Untrustworthy as historian or as a judge of men, the man who can find no more descriptive epithet for Robespierre than "sea-green," or for Marat than "dog-leech," and who could defend Governor Eyre's Jamaica Massacre (in which he had the unfortunate backing of Tennyson and Kingsley), and (quoting his own words, incorrect as regards Mazzini) "utterly unacquainted with the true relation of things in this world," I still regard admiringly the author of *Sartor Resartus*, of *Past and Present*, and of *Hero-Worship*: books which did immense good, coming at a time in which they were expressly wanted, stirring young souls with higher aims than were deducible from socialistic materialisms, or from the Manchester morality of a generation of Whig utilitarians. Very great, I take it, was the service done by Carlyle's earlier books to the young men of that day, giving to them an ennobling gospel, for which England may well hold the Sage of Chelsea in continued reverence. He led the young aristocracy to a clearer perception of the condition of the country and to some recognition of their duties as an aristocracy. He was really the founder of the Disraelitish "Young England" party, a party I would not discredit, though it was not the young England I hoped to see.

CHAPTER XV

Leigh Hunt and his Family; On the *Spectator;* Going to Miteside; The *Leader;* Thornton Hunt; G. H. Lewes; Larken; W. E. Forster; Minter Morgan; Lausanne; Mazzini; Herzen; Lamennais; Forbes; George Combe; Robert Owen.

KNOWING Leigh Hunt, I also knew his family. Hunt had, as so many men of his time also had, imbibed the negative principles of the Frenchmen of 1789. To be free meaned to dispute the justice of established law and to ignore the worth of tradition. This should be borne in mind in judging such men as Shelley, Hunt, and others. The lawlessness of Self-will as a rightful rebellion against the despotism of Authority came to be considered almost as a duty, at least a necessity of courageous free thought. With men of high natures and innate nobleness, their own consciences and wills might be sufficient rulers. Hunt, a man of amiable disposition, good and pure, a Bayard *sans peur* and *sans reproche*, had his conduct little affected by " free " thinking. At worst it left him with a childish carelessness of pecuniary obligations, and also to a considerable disregard of misconstruction. He went on his quiet, pleasurable way, never outraging Mrs. Grundy in his private life, not unconcerned at world-wrongs, speaking honestly but with kindness of all men, and fairly earning his

reputation as "the gentlest of the wise." But his
family, perhaps spoiled by his easiness, inherited that
easiness rather than the chivalrousness which had
kept him free from blame. He had eight children,
sons and daughters. Of his daughters, Florimel, the
eldest, Mrs. Gliddon, was a handsome woman ; Julia,
the second daughter, a *petite* and pretty coquette ;
Jacintha, whom her father used to call " monkey-
face," was the good wife of one of my pupils who,
forsaking engraving, got his living by literature. Of
two of the sons, Percy and Henry, government clerks,
I knew but little, nor cared to know more. It was
perhaps when seeking to get an appointment for one
of them that, it was said, Leigh Hunt and Sheridan
Knowles (the dramatist) met on the steps of the
Government Office and Hunt made way for Knowles,
who was on a like errand, to enter first, with the
remark that there might be only place for one.
John Hunt, the eldest son, though a man not without brains, may have had some mental weakness to
excuse his conduct. After breakfasting with a friend,
he would borrow a book and pledge it at the nearest
pawnbroker's ; he would try to borrow money in his
father's name from his father's friends, on one awk-
ward occasion the father being in the house at which
he called; such like tricks were not infrequent. Vincent, the youngest, was a very lovable fellow ; for
some time employed by me, he wrote for the *Illustrated Family Journal* short, graceful sketches of
wild flowers, somewhat in the style of the father and

possibly helped by him. A weak repeat of his father, gentle but without moral fibre, he died almost before reaching manhood. Thornton, the second son, I knew best, a man rather below average height, deserving rather than his sister the name of " monkey-face," but bright, clever, and very winning, a man in spite of his physiognomy who had his way with women; far too much so, it was notorious, with the pretty wife of his friend George Henry Lewes, the two men only quarreling over the expense of the double family. Thornton asserted his belief in communistic principles, and in self-will as sufficient law. I note him as an instance of what such a man may be in spite of kindly and generous impulses, in spite of great sincerity and straightforwardness, for which traits I could not but like him before I knew him so thoroughly as to lose respect for him.

One instance of real kind-heartedness I may give. He was editor, under the proprietor and manager, Rintoul, of the *Spectator*, a newspaper which, in the words of Carlyle, was at that time " the best article of the kind to be found anywhere in England." One day Thornton interrupted my engraving at Hatton-Garden with a request that I would leave it and come to him, to be for a short time sub-editor with him, in order to keep the place open for a young friend who had been in that capacity and who had fallen sick. I went, partly to oblige Thornton, partly for the sake of the sick man, with whom I had some acquaintance, and partly because I thought, as the call upon my time was only for a few hours on certain days, that it might be worth while to learn something of the management of such a paper. So I took my place for three weeks. At the end of the time Rintoul asked me to dine with him and insisted on paying me for my service, assuring me that the young man now recovered should receive his salary as if he had not been absent. This must have been early in 1849, as during my brief sub-editorship I wrote for the *Spectator* a notice of David Scott, who died on the 5th of March in that year.

In May, 1849, I went to Cumberland, sending my household goods by sea to Whitehaven, and taking my family by steamer (a stormy voyage of nearly three days) to Newcastle; thence across the country by rail to Carlisle and Whitehaven; and from White-haven the sixteen or more miles to my new dwelling-place at " Miteside " by carriage, as the house was some way off the rail line between Whitehaven and Ravenglass. Near Gosforth we had a view of Scaw-fell and the surrounding mountains at the head of Wast-water, some four or five miles from our road. It was a bright Spring day, the road-sides were lined with primroses, in the distance were the dark grey mountains, and between them and the sunlit prim-roses was a fleeting snow-shower. We found our packages of household goods awaiting us, and with them a parcel of reindeer tongues sent by a friend in Newcastle. Bread and milk we got from a farm-house almost adjoining our own; tired out, we slept that night on the floor; and so fairly started on an economical but not too hard life in the strange land. We had a square walled garden on an island in the little river Mite, almost under a line of fells, and from the front of the house we should have seen the sea but for an intervening rise of ground. Ravenglass, about three miles from us, where the Whitehaven railway then terminated, was our nearest town, or rather village; here was the confluence of the Mite and Irt, in which latter stream the Romans fished for the pearl-mussel. I rested here, doing such little engraving as came to me from London, and enjoying the wild beauty of the country. But I was soon called back to London. Some correspondence with Thornton Hunt resulted in our projecting a weekly newspaper, the *Leader*. We found a papermaker and a printer to give help; W. E. Forster (afterwards Secretary for Ireland) took shares in the venture; we had also help from Minter Morgan, a friend of Robert Owen, a man of means who busied himself with a mild sort of socialistic scheme to establish " Happy Villages " under the auspices of the parochial clergy; but the principal funds were contributed by the Rev. Edmund Larken, a friend of Hunt and a " Christian Socialist " of the stamp of Maurice and Kingsley. Larken had married a daughter of Lord Monson, and his rectory was pleasantly situated in his father-in-law's park at Burton, three miles from Lincoln.

My purpose was to make the *Leader* at once an

organ of the European Republicans and the centre of an English republican party after the manner of the *National* and *Réforme* in Paris. So, mindful of even the *Spectator's* insufficient information as regarded European views and happenings, before beginning the newspaper I went to Lausanne, where I expected to find Mazzini, in Switzerland since the fall of Rome, hoping through him to obtain trustworthy foreign correspondents. This was in February, 1850. I had snow the whole way traveling from Dijon to Geneva by the *malle-poste,* with one companion, in a sort of unwheeled cab acting as a sledge. A splendid sight was the rosy dawn lighting the snow as we crossed the Jura Alps, a passage sometimes cut through the snow for us. I reached Geneva about 2 P.M., after a twenty-fours' travel from Dijon, and went to bed; but before I was asleep was ordered out by a buxom chambermaid, so that the bed might be properly made; got up at 10 P.M. to a breakfast or dinner or supper (it might be called either), of twenty dishes, and at midnight left Geneva by diligence for Lausanne, arriving there at about 6 next morning. My hotel was opposite to where the diligence stopped. I breakfasted, and when daylight came sauntered through the streets. Presently my glance rested on another saunterer, whom I guessed to be an Italian. I accosted him, got into some sort of half-understood conversation with him, and at last won so much upon his confidence as to learn where I might hear of Mazzini. There I went, only to be told that a letter could be forwarded to him, which sent, in an hour I had an appointment to see him. I spent a week in Lausanne, daily with him and Saffi, who was in the same house. There were many Italian and French refugees in the city, Felix Pyat among the French, who seemed to me much inferior in appearance and bearing to the Italians. When I came away, I had for companion an Englishman, Colonel Hugh Forbes, who had come out of Rome with Garibaldi, and who, when Garibaldi divided his forces, had commanded one division. I brought away letters from Mazzini, and tracts to be distributed in Paris. The tracts were bound together in a thick volume with a title-page of one of Gioberti's unobjectionable works. When at the frontier, we were ordered out of the diligence for examination, I left the volume open at the title-page on my seat, and it escaped suspicion. At Lyons we breakfasted, and thence went on to Paris, where we spent the next day. Here I had the happiness of a cordial meeting with dear old Lamennais (not to be seen again), and a welcome from Herzen, the Russian friend to whom Mazzini had given me an introduction, and of whom I shall have to speak again. Most of the day else we passed in the company of Madame Bourdillon Nassy (whom I had known in England as Eliza Ashurst, an early translator of some of George Sand's novels) and her husband. By them I was introduced to Maria Weston Chapman, American and Abolitionist, a very beautiful woman. Forbes and I dined with the Nassys, and left Paris by the evening train for Calais. At Calais it was a dark and stormy night, the pier was being repaired, and the English steamer could not put in to it. I scrambled down the side of the pier into a boat; but Forbes was not quick enough in following me; and the boat was full and went off without him. It was pitch-dark, the sea rough, the boatmen were saying their prayers; and I had some fear that, unable to find the steamer, we might have to go back, and not without danger. But at length we reached a black mass, which was our ship. Forbes was left behind; and no other steamer crossed the channel for forty-eight hours, the weather being so bad. I got safely to London, and reported to Larken at the Rectory, resting there pleasantly for some days. Forbes crossed so soon as the weather allowed; but I did not see him, as he left England for America directly. He afterwards returned to Europe, to take part in Garibaldi's Sicilian expedition.

The *Leader* was started: Hunt as principal editor and manager, Lewes as literary editor, myself taking the place of editor for foreign matters, and Ballantyne for English. Ballantyne had been on the Manchester *Examiner*. He and I worked together, and very agreeably; but I had soon to find that Hunt's and Lewes' sympathies with the republican party were not to be depended on, that they merely wanted to exploit the connection for the commercial advantage of the paper. After a few weeks I gave up my position. I recollect but one meeting toward the formation of a party, and but one person of any prominence at that — George Combe, who gave us an amusing account of Robert Owen's impracticability at his American colony, "New Harmony." Coleridge's button-holding Lamb till Lamb cut off the button and left him to discourse to that, was but a type of Owen's never-ending and never-varying speech. On occasion of the first meeting at New Harmony, his oration had to be interrupted with the important question, " Pardon me, Mr. Owen, but I would ask if any here can milk a cow? If so, let them hold up their hands, for the cows can not wait for oratory." I had plenty of opportunity for observing this as characteristic of Owen, a most dry and unimaginative creature, who, like his son, Robert Dale (whom I afterwards met in New York, a man far cleverer and in every way more capable than the father), finished not unnaturally with a blind subservience to "spiritualism." Extremes meet.

So much for the *Leader*, which led nowhither, under the capricious direction of Hunt and Lewes, running, like Leigh Hunt's Irishman's pig, "up all manner of streets." Disappointed in it, and feeling that my republican friends had also cause for disappointment, I undertook a work which occupied me for nearly five years, the publication of the *English Republic*.

CHAPTER XVI

The English Republic; The Plaint of Freedom; Walter Savage Landor; Duffy; Carlyle; Joseph Cowen; Other Helpers; *Deceased British Painters* and other Work; Moxon; Visitors and Friends; Physicians.

My object, plainly avowed, in bringing out the *English Republic* was "to explain Republican Principles, to record Republican Progress, and to establish a Republican Party in England." The record of progress would of course include notices of republican happenings everywhere. My work began with 1851, a monthly magazine, at first printed at Leeds, in the hope of there taking up some of the subscribers to the *Present Age*, a serious, liberal magazine edited by Dr. F. R. Lees, the head of the Temperance agitation. The expected advantage on both sides not arriving, the *Present Age* was discontinued and I went on with my own venture, still printing at Leeds, my publisher in London my old friend James Watson. At the same time I pursued my engraving, such as I could have at that distance from London, both for support of my family and to pay for my republican endeavour. I was also writing for the *Nation*, chiefly "rhymes and reasons" concerning the one great Irish difficulty, the Land Question; and in 1852 I printed at Newcastle and put out anonymously (why so it would be hard to say, unless it was that I doubted my own ability for writing so serious a work) a long poem, *The Plaint of Freedom*, of which I gave away the whole edition of three hundred. I had many satisfactory acknowledgments, the best from Walter Savage Landor, to whom I was indebted for occasional writing in the *English Republic*. Before he knew the poem was mine, he wrote the following lines, which I may dare to quote (I had dedicated the poem " to the memory of Milton," with farther notice of him):—

"To the Author of the Plaint of Freedom.

"Praiser of Milton! worthy of *his* praise!
  How shall I name thee? Art thou yet unnamed?
  While verses flourish hanging overhead
  In looser tendrils than stern husbandry
  May well approve, on thee shall none descend?
  At Milton's hallow'd name thy hymn august
  Sounds as the largest bell from Minster tower.
  I ponder, and in time may dare to praise;
  Milton had done it; Milton would have graspt
  Thy hand amid his darkness, and with more
  Impatient pertinacity because
  He heard the voice and could not see the face."

He sent me the lines later (when he knew the poem was mine) with his volume, *The Last Fruit of an Old Tree*, and with a letter, which I am proud enough to subjoin:—

"Bath, Nov. 8, 1852.

"My Dear Sir.

"This morning I send to you by railway my new volume. I left a quantity of writing to the disposal of Mr. Forster, and

I regret that he has not inserted lines I addrest to you. I was not aware of this until the volume was bound and sent to me. If there is anything in the volume which your pure and exquisite taste approves, I shall be more gratified than by all the Reviewers and Magazine-men, even if any of them (which is improbable) should commend it.

> "Very truly yours,
> "W. S. LANDOR."

He printed the lines afterwards in 1858, in the *Dry Sticks, fagoted by W. S. Landor*, his last book.

In 1853 he sent me his volume, the *Imaginary Conversations of Greeks and Romans* (republished in that year by Moxon) with the flattering ascription: —

> "W. S. Landor to W. J. Linton,
> A true patriot and a true poet,
> Characters almost equally rare."

Surely encouragement enough was this for a lone endeavourer, beside the cordial help of Mazzini and his fellow-republicans, and the warm and friendly reception I had from Duffy in the Irish *Nation*. Carlyle, too, would sometimes acknowledge the copies of the *Republic* (which I regularly sent to him) with not unfriendly characteristic growl, which did not disconcert but rather amused me from a man so averse to windiness, so ready to preach the worthlessness of words. Why waste my energy in useless speech? — was the one burden of his remonstrances, and he would not have cared had I pleaded the influence of his example. Like him, I was bound to speak, without the warrant of his genius, but with a more prophetic hope. I failed. Some words may yet have echoes. Some few feeble attempts at republican association of a few working-men, in response to a plan of action from which I looked for results, showed me that I might teach, but might not lead. I stood almost alone. One man, a young lawyer at Eastbourne, now residing at Matlock, Derbyshire, whose friendship I have kept ever since, sent me ten pounds to help me in my work, — the only money subscribed to me except by Joseph Cowen, who helped me generously and largely until I had to abandon my work. In the writing he had no part.

In 1852 and 1853 the *Republic* was issued in four-page weekly tracts, bound together for monthly parts, still printed at Leeds. In the spring of 1852 I removed to Brantwood, and in 1854 resumed the monthly issue, by then having printing press and types, and registering myself as a printer, without which my printing material was liable to seizure and confiscation by the authorities. At Brantwood I had the assistance of three young men from Chel-tenham, who came across the country to offer them-selves at my service, at any wage that I could afford them. Two were printers, and the third was a gardener. They were zealous and efficient helpers. When, in April, 1855, I had to give up the endeavour (it had never reached a paying point, and of the few hundreds printed many were distributed freely in the hope of propagandism), my three men had to leave me: one went back to Cheltenham, his native place, resumed printing there, and established a printing-office noteworthy for its excellent work; one found employment for a time in London, and has now for many years been the editor of the weekly edition of Mr. Cowen's *Newcastle Chronicle*; one returned to gardening and has been long in the employment of a gentleman in the neighbourhood of London: all fairly well doing, all to this day my attached and esteemed friends, none ever complaining of lost time at Brantwood. Their names, not among the candidates for notoriety, are written on my heart.

At Brantwood, as at Miteside, my literary work being unremunerative, I continued my engraving, fortunate in being engaged by the Art Union of London to execute a series of cuts after the works of *Deceased British Painters*, some from my own drawings. I had also occasional work for the *Illustrated London News*, and some from drawings by Rossetti, Millais, Stanfield, Creswick, and others, for Moxon's edition of Tennyson's *Poems*. And here I may record a piece of generous kindness, not, so far as my own experience went, too common among publishers. It was at Brantwood; and I was one day standing at an outer gate, when, unexpected, I saw Moxon coming. I had such illness in my house that I could not even ask him to come in, but stood at the gate to answer his inquiry as to the progress of his work. I was in arrear and could give no definite promise of performance.   He was considerately indulgent, wished me good morning and turned away; then, a few paces gone, turned back to say, with kindly hesitation, that he knew artists were not a moneyed race, and under present circumstances would I allow him to act as a friend, offering me a ten-pound note which, he said, was more than he would want for the little time he was traveling through the Lake Country. I gratefully took the advanced payment.

Poor Moxon! his book, owing to the war between North and South in America, which disappointed him of a large sale, was a failure; and the failure, I believe, ruined his business. He was one of those publishers who are patrons of literature, taking interest in his books, and so — associated with their authors — a publisher worthy of honour.

Half a mile or but a little more to the railway, by boat across the Lake (to Coniston Hall, once the seat of Sidney's sister, Ben Jonson's Countess of Pembroke), or a three miles' walk round the Waterhead, my engraving went by rail from Church Coniston at 7 P.M., to be delivered in London as soon as houses of business were open next morning, so that I was hardly out of the way for those publishers who still knew me and valued what I did. Nor was I altogether without visitors and friends; Mr. Gibson, our valued Coniston and Hawkshead doctor (Hawkshead, where Wordsworth went to school in the grammar school there, four miles from Coniston, at

K

the head of Esthwaite Water), Dr. Lonsdale of Carlisle, our neighbours the Misses Romney (two maiden
ladies, grand-daughters of the painter), Harriet Martineau, Dr. Lees, Wm. Bridges Adams, Richard Tyas
(an old lawyer friend of many years), Joseph Cowen,
Wm. Bell Scott, Edward Wehnert, Duncan, and some
others.   Harriet Martineau lived at Ambleside, ten
miles from us, not too far to be visited or to visit us.
Lees and other friends from a distance were introduced to our mountains, and for entertainment had
rambles over them.   Lees, a determined teetotaler
and, I think, the most learned of the race, was free
enough not to disallow our stopping at a country inn
after a long tramp; and confessed, to my asking,
that it would be of little use to lecture against
whiskey in that moist realm of meres and waters.
Duncan, the most accurate of draftsmen, whose true
realism stood him in the place of imagination, once
spent a week with me tracking the River Duddon
from the sea to its mountain source, taking sketches
which we hoped might turn to account as illustrations to Wordsworth's *Sonnets on the Duddon;* but,
when we came to consider poems and sketches
together, we found that the *Sonnets,* ecclesiastical
and other, were pure Wordsworth, and might as well
have been written on any other river.   Then in time
of need Dr. Lietch of Keswick would come thirty
miles to give his unfee'd service; and good Dr. Brown
of Blaydon-on-Tyne came across the country, a day's
journey, on the same generous errand, — so keeping

up the medical tradition I had learned in London, where, when I had scarlet fever, three doctors stood together at my bedside, Toynbee, the Quaker Dr. Hodgkin, and Southwood Smith, the last attending me through my illness. I never paid a physician's fee in England. Only on Dr. Sibson I had some claim for sake of his brother, my artist friend; and the doctor honoured my claim by gratuitous advice to any one I chose to send to him. In one man so sent he became so interested that for years afterwards, until his patient's death, Sibson was at his service whenever required. I may be grateful and proud for such services, yet I do not take all the credit to myself, but recognise them as fair instances of the generosity of the medical profession in England toward artists and literary men.

CHAPTER XVII

My Possessions ; Stolzman ; To the Top of Scawfell.

At Brantwood I rented a garden between the house and the Lake, and had another small garden patch, with bees, reached by steps to above the height of the house. From this patch was a view across the Lake to the "Old Man" and Coniston Crags under Wetherlam ; and from the lower garden we looked up the Lake to Helvellyn. I had the use of a horse, and kept two cows, a pig, pigeons, and poultry (an occasional pheasant would breakfast with my chickens), and some twenty sheep ; my cows pasturing in two fields between the house and Lake (two fields rented with the garden), my sheep feeding on the fell, which rose some three or four hundred feet steeply, directly behind the house, the side of the fell covered with copse wood, young oak, and hazel. On one part, not so brant (*i.e.*, steep), I felled the larger oak, barked it (much with my own hands), and sold the bark ; then, perhaps for the first time ever done, had an acre or more ploughed, and corn and garden stuff raised upon it. My sheep-feeding on the fell above entitled me, when the common land between Coniston Water and

Esthwaite Water was enclosed, to an apportionment of six acres, mostly covered with heather and juniper, so that I had sixteen acres instead of ten to sell to Ruskin.

I knew every mountain pass in the square of the Lake Country, some thirty miles each way; and many were the rambles, of a day or of two, three, four, or more days, through the country, with friend, or friends, or alone. It was a life worth having. My Polish friend Stolzman came in 1852 to live with me, and helped to teach my three boys. He was with me till 1854; then, ailing, went for change to the sea, at Haverhill, under Black Combe. He had just been elected to the Polish Central Democratic Committee, and was anxious to recover some strength for his work in that, and for a possible return to Poland, if England, in the war then threatened, could be wise enough to attack Russia in the North. At Haverhill he had a paralytic fit, and in three hours was dead. I reached his side only in time to see him buried in the little churchyard of Millom, the incumbent of which, waiting my arrival, had charitably made the funeral arrangements. For ten years I knew Stolzman. I have known none more worthy of friendship and honour than the old soldier exile.

That life in the North was indeed worth living, though heavy sorrow came to me there, which caused my return to London after my discontinuance of the *English Republic* in 1855.

One day's excursion, well recollected, may be

worth recording here from memoranda written at the time : the excursion, however, not taken while I was living at Brantwood, but on occasion of revisiting the country some years afterwards. I had gone with some friends from Keswick to Buttermere, and they left me at Buttermere, where I slept. Next day, it is a fair June day, the twentieth of the month, crossing over Honistar Pass, where the slate quarries are, I reach, soon after noon, little Seathwaite, on the near side of the Borrowdale road. After the best meal I can get, bread and cheese and milk, I take it into my head that I will pass midsummer eve on the top of Scawfell, the highest ground in England. I go over Stockley Bridge, and follow the beck, up the gorge, taking a bath on my way. It is steep climbing for some hours, occasionally looking back over the length of Borrowdale for a distant view of Derwent Water and the line of Skiddaw and Blencathra ; and, as I rise higher, catching sight of Langdale Pikes, bright and glowing as they pierce into the sunshine. Then, rounding Great End, a bulwark of Scawfell, a long shoulder is before me, in front of which is Scawfell itself, to my left a sea of mountains, to my right Great Gable gradually lost, as I advance, in the shadow of the End. I reach the top of the shoulder to find that the End has slipped away, leaving me to climb an empty sleeve in which he was laughing at me ; and the End is as far off as ever, and Scawfell top seeming at greater distance. Another steep climb, with right below me a seemingly bottomless pit; but a little farther on a green platform rises in the pit, in the middle of which is Sty Head Tarn, shining like an emerald. A quarter of a mile of scrambling over a sea of rocks; and then Scawfell looks nearer, but bigger and more formidable than ever. As I proceed he grows, ever more and more gigantic, till I am at the very foot of his own shoulder (as an Irishman might say, and very correctly). Before attempting that last climb, I look over the lower heights, and see a lake of gold, Ennerdale Water, lying in the grey, formless mist beyond them. Then I begin to ascend the shoulder, up steep, loose stones, digging places for my feet as I mount, not without fear of bringing down upon me an avalanche of slates and boulders. At last I am on the summit, still among the stones, but with one patch of golden moss among them, which I pass to the pole like a flag-staff on the topmost height of the Pike, and of all England.

On the broad platform are some broken walls, the remains of huts built for the Ordnance Surveyors; I choose one with part of a chimney in it, the walls nearly as high as my head, and prepare to take my rest so half sheltered. The distances are growing dim, lost in haze; but before sunset some clearing brings out far Derwent Water (or is it farther Bassenthwaite Water?) in full brightness; to my right Windermere lights up; the sea is behind me; and the passing sunlight glances warmly on the pile of stones on which the pole is set, and on the ruined walls of my chamber, till the sun sinks, leaving long bars of crimson and gold, and a tender mellow glory over everything.   One last look at the flag-staff where it stands alone against the pure sky, the young crescent moon, clear as crystal, rising in the pale after-glow of the sunset; then, as the stars come out one by one, I lie down in my half-chimnied room, against a broken wall, and watch the white clouds floating silently over me till I fall asleep in the lingering twilight.   Awaking, the stars are gone; all is a dead mist; I see only the grey walls, and hear the winds careering overhead.   By and by the mist thins enough to show the light of the sun's path as he travels northward, yet far from dawn.   That light never leaves the sky all night, only for a time lost in the mist.   The expanse of mist changes to slight misty clouds rapidly driven across the sky, rather mists in motion than anything in shape of cloud; the light in the horizon extends eastward and increases; some faint tinge of scarcely colour comes into it, ripening to the vague colouring of a sea-shell, to a faint red, to reddish gold, to golden brown, to golden red, to deeper red, and pure gold.   The mountain-tops appear in grey, slowly warming to a greenish tone in the nearer ones, the distance still grey.   Northward the line of cloud in which the sun had set extends itself in long bars, becoming more distinct, darker, and seeming nearer.   Out of this line comes a little black cloud, coming nearer, nearer, and then suddenly melting away.   The mountains beyond Windermere lie in long lines of grey, with mist between, and behind their ranges. Behind the mist rise strange black, heavy monsters, coming close in their blackness through the intervening mass of mist miles away, sometimes like a herd of buffaloes leaping over one another, sometimes one gigantic beast about to tumble over the wall. Higher in the western sky are great wind-formed feathers. Then the dawn grows light, colours are more distinct, the sky is streaked and golden. It is still misty over Skiddaw and the long cloud-arms threaten to travel eastward and hide the sunrise ; and behind me clouds are sweeping up from the near sea. Afraid of being lost in the mists, I begin to descend. But a little way down, the great ball of fire bursts out for one glorious moment, purpling the dark crags and making the clouds rosy and coppery, then losing itself in the crimson clouds above. I hasten down the opposite way to that I had climbed, to Wastdale Head, breakfast there, and mid driving rain make my way over Sty Head Pass, the wildest pass of the English mountains, to Borrowdale, and through Borrowdale to Derwent Water and Keswick.

CHAPTER XVIII

The Poles at Liverpool; Meeting at Hanover Square; Herzen; Bakounine.

IT was in 1849 that the Hungarian war for freedom came to an unhappy end, through the insolent intervention of Russia aided by the treachery of Görgey, the Hungarian General; and Kossuth, with the last hopes of patriotism, took refuge under the hospitality of the Sultan. In March, 1851 (I was then living at Miteside), two hundred and sixty-one of these men, the remnant of the Polish Legion which had fought under General Wysocki, the last of 1034 who had taken refuge in Turkey in 1849, arrived at Liverpool from Kutayeh. There were two hundred and forty-seven Poles: the rest were of different nationalities, nine of them Hungarians. On reaching the Mersey their vessel was boarded by a Mr. Diosy, a Hungarian and emigration agent, deputed by the Literary Society of the Friends of Poland, with the object of persuading the refugees to accept a free passage to America, offered them by the British Government as the best means of getting rid of them. The Poles, already in communication with their countryman Mr. Worcell, the chief of the Polish Emigration, refused to be so deported. Worcell had come from London to meet them, and I had joined him to be of what service I could to him and them. I tried to make interest for them, and called upon Robertson Gladstone, James Martineau, and other prominent men in Liverpool, but without effect. We then appealed to a public meeting; with difficulty found an " influential " chairman, and put the case before the meeting of nearly all working-men. In spite of some " respectable " opposition, in spite of false statements circulated through the Liverpool Press, the meeting was successful; volunteers, work-ing-men, came forward offering individual help : one man would take to his home and care for one of the refugees; another man would take one more, and a committee was formed for farther combined efforts.

At first the strangers were lodged in a house allowed them by the Authorities; but they were quickly informed that they would be ejected unless they accepted the Government terms. On the 12th of March, two days after our public meeting (they only landed on the 4th) they were accordingly turned into the streets. One generous man, Mr. Peter Stewart, a Liverpool merchant, was found to get them admission to an unused soap-factory, or they had been houseless. My poor friend Worcell was too feeble from sickness to do more than direct, and I had to act for him, with the aid of a young Pole, who spoke French but could not speak or understand English. The soap-factory was in a back street in Liverpool, the room large enough, but quite bare, up a narrow flight of stairs. A rough crowd surrounded the door at the foot of the stairs as two hundred and thirty men passed in. An active friend, a Liverpool man, and an old chartist, got them a supply of straw, but there was no water in the place. I appealed to the crowd. "What will you pay?" "Nothing!" explaining the circumstances, " and you must bring your own pails." " I will "— said one woman in the crowd. "I will "— said another. So we got water enough, allowing the bringers to go up-stairs to look at the strangers, which seemed to be considered a reward. At midnight, before leaving for home, I took a last look at the two hundred and thirty lying in rows on the floor, with one sentinel walking to and fro among them, so that no one should come in. So I left them to the action of the Committee on the morrow. Mr. Stewart sent them £50 and gifts of vegetables ; biscuit, owing to a short voyage from Kutayeh, they had in plenty, which we stored in a Temperance Hotel, kept by a political sympathiser. Of this biscuit the Custom House (the very officers ashamed of what they had to do) took as duty ten per cent, weighing it on the quay as it was landed. Never was I more ashamed of my country than when I stood upon that quay, and had to place a cordon of men to prevent the poor starvelings, Irish and others, about the docks, from also stealing their percentage. As the biscuit was being uncarted at the hotel, I noticed two villainous-looking fellows hanging about, evidently with intent to steal anything in their way.

I asked them what they were there for, and had of course a rough and saucy answer. I told them in few words who and what the refugees were, and how, unable to speak English, they were in a worse condition than any Englishmen could be; and my two villains replied that I need not be afraid of them, and walked down the street with me to ask farther questions.

Our Liverpool Committee worked well; other Committees were formed elsewhere; the Poles were gradually drafted to different parts of the country, some obtaining employment of one sort, some of another. They waited in vain for another chance for Polish service; and all may not eventually have remained in England; but I never heard complaint of any one of them, and with some I had opportunities for personal knowledge and personal regard.

But I was ashamed of the influential " liberals " of Liverpool, and ashamed, not for the first time, of the then " liberal " government of England. Two years later, these dispersed patriots should have been wanted for the Crimean War.

The promise of war, again giving hope to Poland, brought together the refugees in London, to a public meeting at the Hanover Square Rooms, on the 29th of November, 1853, to celebrate the thirty-third anniversary of the Polish Insurrection. It was the first open recognition of English republicanism in accord with European; and the first public gathering of representatives of European nationalities in

Poland's name and their own to demand help from England, and to proclaim on English soil the necessity of a new campaign against the unholy Alliance of Kings. Mr. Worcell, as chief of the Polish Central Committee, took the chair. He was too feeble to speak, and I had to read for him the Address of the Committee in English, also read by others in Polish and French. Then Herzen spoke for Russia and Russian sympathy with Poland. He was followed by me, and then by Dr. Arnold Ruge, the German member of the European Committee, speaking in German. Dr. Paul Darasz, the brother of Albert Darasz (but lately dead, who had been one of the first members of Mazzini's European Committee), spoke in French; and Dr. Ronay, a Hungarian, addressed the English part of the audience in their own tongue, and then, turning to the Poles and Hungarians, spoke to them in Latin. Then two letters were read from Mazzini, who was too ill to be able to attend the meeting: one in English, one in French read by Colonel Pianciani, who also added his own speech in French. Thomas Cooper said a few words for English working-men; Ledru Rollin was eloquent in French; and the proceedings closed in English from a Pole, M. Staniewicz. It was a large and enthusiastic meeting, an anticipatory protest against the mismanagement of that unhappy and useless Crimean War, and notable as a promise of alliance of the peoples, some day yet perhaps to result in action, however unnoticed then.

Something I may here say of the men who took part in the meeting. Of Worcell I have already spoken, and shall have to speak again. Dr. Paul Darasz was a Polish physician, who escaped from a Russian prison to England to join his brother Albert, then dying from consumption. Albert Darasz, born at Warsaw in 1808, and distinguished in the Polish Insurrection of 1830, had been in exile one of the most active of the Polish Democrats. Expelled from France because concerned in Ledru Rollin's manifestation against Louis Napoleon's attack on Rome, he came to London, there joining Mazzini on the Central European Committee, and there dying on the 19th of September, 1852. Arnold Ruge, another exile, who had been of the party of Struve and Hecker and Robert Blum, the republican party in the unfortunate Frankfort Parliament, lived many years in England, a man of literary ability and very much respected. Dr. Ronay, a small, slight man, with the look of a clergyman, I knew only as a Hungarian refugee. Pianciani, a tall man of soldierly bearing, with a face scarred by gunpowder, was one of the most faithful and devoted of the Mazzinians. He fell, I believe, some years later, in one of the many attempts for Italian freedom. Ledru Rollin, the eloquent parliamentarian, but true beyond any parliamentarism, is too well known to need words of mine. M. Staniewicz, an old Polish insurrectionist of 1830, had since 1831 been resident in England. Of Alexander Herzen, the Russian, there is more to be said.

High-born, of a family in the highest social position, the boy Herzen entered the University of Moscow, there to hear the unforgotten name of Pestel,
and among the youth of the University to dream of
some yet possible change in Russia, — to dream of
it and perhaps to talk with some want of reserve.
When only just of age, in 1834, he was arrested (as
Mazzini and so many others were in the despotic
countries of Europe) on the all-sufficient suspicion of
having a patriotic disposition, and after nearly a
year's imprisonment was sentenced to banishment to
the eastern confines of Russia, there to be employed
in a government office, under the eyes of the police:
to be so kept out of mischief, and perhaps recovered
from the threatened error of his way. The office,
using his own words, " was worse than the prison."
However, he fulfilled his duties there and, found to
have exceptional talent, was at length given some
sort of promotion, and after a time allowed to
approach the neighbourhood of Moscow, still under
the *surveillance* of the police. With some personal
liberty he stole a visit to Moscow, where he married
a cousin to whom he had been engaged before his
banishment; and in 1839, his father being wealthy
and influential, he got leave to go to Petersburg, and
to be tempted with a place in the office for the Minister for Home Affairs.

Again he seems to have been not careful enough
in speech; and now with a remarkable mixture of
threat and bribe, he was given the office of Council-

lor to the Regency of Novgorod, and ordered to his duties there, still watched by the police. Powerful friends at last obtained leave for him to resign and return to Moscow. This was in 1842. By his father's death he now became a rich man, and appeared to be content with a studious life. Years passed in vain endeavours of friends at Court to gain permission for him to travel; and it was only in 1847 that, on account of his wife's health, he was given a passport that he might visit the German baths. Once across the Russian frontier, he was free, and refused to return. The Tzar would have confiscated his estates but was estopped, Herzen's first care having been to sell them to one Rothschild for an annuity.

With Mazzini's introduction, I had made Herzen's acquaintance in Paris in 1850. In 1852 he came to England and we became friends. He came to London in order to found, with the help of his Polish compatriots, a free Russian Press. He was already favourably known by an important work written in French, *On the Development of Revolutionary Ideas in Russia.* Hearty assistance was rendered him by the Poles, who had already their printing office in London, and with their propagandist help also his first serial paper, the *Kolokol* (the *Alarm Bell*), and later the *Polar Star* (a name recalling a former publication by Ryléieff and Bestoujeff, the companions of Pestel) were spread throughout Russia, reaching even to the palace of the Tzar. Herzen was the one rich man of the knot of European revolutionists at

L

that time in London. For some time he lived in a pleasant country mansion, Elmfield House, at Teddington, by the side of the Thames. I remember being there on the day the news came of the death of the Tzar Nicholas. The rooms were crowded with political friends, Russians, Poles, Frenchmen, Germans, Italians, and English, all sharing in Herzen's joy, which was unbounded and almost savage. Later, in 1857, he and I, with Ledru Rollin and Mazzini, were fellow-mourners at the grave of Worcell, Mazzini's dearest friend, dear also to all who came within his sphere. There, when the coffin had to be carried from the chapel to the grave, Herzen rose from his seat, tears falling down his cheeks, and took his place as one of the bearers. It was at once a token of affection for his friend, and of homage to the patriot Pole.

In person Herzen was short of stature, stoutly built, in his last days inclined to corpulence, with a grand head, long chestnut hair and beard, small, luminous eyes, and rather ruddy complexion. Suave in his manner, courteous, but with an intense power of irony, witty, choice as well as ready in speech, clear, concise, and impressive, he was a subtle and profound thinker, with all the passionate nature of the "barbarian," yet generous and humane. He died at Paris on the 21st of January, 1870, leaving a son, since become a physician, and two younger daughters of whom he was passionately fond.

I knew him well, having the opportunity of much personal and friendly intercourse with him. He wrote for me on Russia, in my *English Republic*. He was helpful always to the refugees in England, to the Poles as much as to his own countrymen; intimate with Mazzini and Worcell and other chiefs of exile. Hospitable, and taking pleasure in society, he was a good conversationalist, with a frank and pleasant manner. At his table I met Bakounine, the "anarchist," a man to be honoured for his endeavours to bring about a *rapprochement* between the Poles and Russians, an object which Herzen also had much at heart. Bakounine was one of the patriots of '48, on the barricades at Dresden. After the republican failure in that year, he suffered two years in a Saxon prison, then some time in an Austrian, and then, given up by Austria to Russia, was lost for years in a Russian casemate. It was reported that he had been chained by the neck, and that he had died in his prison. But he had been sent to Siberia, whence he escaped to China and passed from there through America to England. I found him a strong-looking man over six feet in height, cheerful and humorous, laughing heartily when I told him of my having written of his life and death.

CHAPTER XIX

Worcell; Mazzini; American Sympathy; Grant.

OF Worcell I have written elsewhere (*European Republicans*, Laurence & Bullen, London, 1892). Here Herzen may speak for me. " He was a Saint, and this word best expresses his dominant characteristic. All that most strikes us in the Legends of the Saints we find in him : trait for trait, with more of love, with a more human element. Of a nature eminently religious, his genius was logically wide-sighted, but at the same time delicately subtle. Highly endowed with the faculty of abstract reasoning, he naturally became a profound mathematician. His active and ardent mind, however, stopped not at geometry and astronomy, but studied in turn all the natural sciences. His erudition was prodigious. Speaking, not only well but elegantly, French, English, and German, he was thoroughly acquainted with modern literature. I often addressed myself to him as a living cyclopedia. Conscientious in everything, if he afterwards thought that he had been wrong, he would next day write in correction. This mass of varied knowledge, with a reflection of that certain mysticism which we always meet with in the Polish poets, gave a peculiar originality to his conversation and to his way of looking at things. And all this, science and mysticism, history and mathematics, was only on the lower plane of his life. Above all was his religion, the thought of his whole existence, his faith in Poland. His whole soul was there, having sacrificed to that cause his home happiness, his fortune, his entire life. He laboured twenty-six years, in exile for the organisation of the Republican party in the Polish Emigration. Overwhelmed with misfortunes, privations, maladies, he was day and night at his work, with that calm serenity, that resigned gentleness, that candid simplicity, which a faith not to be shaken gives to a great heart. No one ever heard a single plaint from his mouth."

I quote from Herzen's *Polar Star*, preferring the words of a man not more intimate with Worcell than I myself was, but better qualified to appreciate him completely. My own recollections entirely confirm Herzen's account.

Poor, always poor, hardly supported by irregular remittances from friends in Poland, his scanty means shared with his yet needier compatriots, I was, while in London, too sadly aware of his poverty and cognizant of his generosity and devotedness. He was a constant sufferer from asthma, and I do not recollect ever seeing him at ease, except on one day, when, some political object calling him from London, he came to see his friend Stolzman and myself at Coniston. There, with some difficulty getting him on the fell at the back of my house, resting on the height, revived by the pure air, he said that he felt like a new man. But weak or sick or in pain he was always ready, at any personal inconvenience, at any risk, to meet the continual calls upon him for advice or exertion, calls from the whole body of the Polish refugees, who looked to him as a wise father. On the same ground I learned to love him, loving him and loved by him to his death, on the 3d of February, 1857.

With the Polish refugees in London, with Mazzini and Ledru Rollin and P. A. Taylor, Jun., the Member of Parliament for Leicester (Worcell's good friend), I followed to his grave in Highgate Cemetery, the grave in which Darasz had been laid four years before. Ledru Rollin and Taylor spoke over it. His epitaph (from which alone I learn his age — I thought he had been much older), with that of Darasz, for a contemplated monument, is before me in the handwriting of Kossuth.

Hic requiescit
quidquid mortale est

ALBERTI DARASZ

Exercitus Poloniensis Litenentis
ex ordine "virtuti militari" equitis
qui
natus anno Christi MDCCCVIII die Augusti XIX
vita decessit exsul
anno MDCCCLII.

Item
STANISLAS WORCELL
qui
anno MDCCXCIX natus
ad Conventus Poloniæ anno illo nostro
MDCCCXXXI publice legatus
pari fato exsul
anno MDCCCLVII die III Februarii
mortuus est

Uterque
patriæ amore ardens
laboris pervicax populo devotus
in aliena quamvis amica terra
viris delectis Poloniensium
multos annos præsidens
pro plebe populoque
Summœ libertati consulebat

Talibus Viris
propter excelsas ipsorum virtutes
propter merita ac labores
publica causa susceptos
socii eorundem exsules
necnon pluribus e gentibus
Jurium Poloniæ suffragatores
sumptu communi
hic monumentum
struxere

Of Mazzini there is little need to speak. His
great career, his genius, his deeds, and his worth, are
written on the scroll of History in characters which
even the inventive pen of Detraction can not now be-

little. He stands, as I believe, the greatest man in this nineteenth century, none greater in the years of Time, the Prophet of the Future. What remains for me to speak of is simply the recollections of his personality and of my own relations with him. I never found change in him, except the change of increased warmth in a growing friendship. His conversation during the five years from 1843 to 1848, the years in which I was oftenest with him, was always frank and wise. On whatever subject he spoke, political, social, or literary (English literature included), there was always something to be learned from him. His greeting was invariably warm and cheerful, his manner that of an affectionate friend, whether in general company, in his own chamber, or in my house among my children. Of children he was fond. Well I recollect one night leaving with him his Italian School at Greville Street, Hatton-Garden, when he lifted in his arms the tired child of an Italian workman, and carried the boy as he would a friend's son. Not merely a leader, even of the great cause of Italian Freedom, his heart was tender toward all sufferers, his disposition compassionate, the disposition of a man who loved. He came to me once with tears in his eyes, telling me of his friend Stolzman, whom he had found starving, because the old soldier would not even of him ask help, knowing the many claims upon him of his Italians. He was a man who had not only the faculty of loving, but also the faculty of inspiring love. Few came under his magnetic influence without becoming attached to him; even those who were unable to comprehend his highest thoughts. Many served him for his own sake, though they might not fully appreciate his faith or feel any real deep interest in his purposes.

Even in America he was not without sympathisers. A young Polish friend, coming to the States, enlisted friends who promised to form for him an Italian party. When I came to America at the end of 1866, Mazzini charged me to bring them together for some reality of active help, and to explain his principles and views. Some of these men were dead, some I spoke with. I need not name them here. They had cooled; they saw nothing to be done, they were too scattered and isolated to be of use. Perhaps I myself did not sufficiently persevere, was not strenuously urgent; but the Italian party melted away, like snow on a warm morning, even as the interest evoked by Kossuth in both England and America had also vanished without effect. There were but few exceptions. Introduced by Wendell Phillips to General Rawlings, then War Secretary, very cordially received by him, and by him taken to Grant, I had the opportunity of speaking with, I ought rather to say of speaking to, the President; was met with enough courtesy, and listened to, but with no appearance of interest or understanding; and came out grieved and disheartened. Certainly there was no help for European Republicanism in democratic America: the utmost stretch of sympathy in the United

States (still I own to some few noble exceptions) producing only occasional cheers for the eloquent orator and a certain tolerance for unfortunate refugees. Enough of a bootless complaint!

CHAPTER XX

Norwood; Colonel Reid; Babbage; Sloman; Cobden; O'Connell; Frances Wright; Owen; Landor; Browning; Oastler; Paxton; Place; Perronet Thompson; P. A. Taylor; Hickson; Ebenezer Elliott; George Dawson; F. W. Newman; J. H. Newman; Epps; Bowring; Dickens; Holyoake; Bradlaugh.

I RETURN to earlier recollections. Norwood I knew before the Crystal Palace was thought of, where indeed was a wood, a rare place for the entomologist, where in my boyish days I made collections of butterflies, dragon-flies and beetles. Of many men and women crossing my path in maturer years, who came "like shadows" and so departed, I can recall the names, but little more. For Colonel Reid, a gaunt Scotchman, the author of the *Law of Storms*, a work which antedated the work of Maury, I did the first engraving on my own account, cuts of wrecks and wind-driven ships, designed by Duncan. With a strange sort of unusual fitness for place, Reid became the governor of the "vexed Bermoothes." Babbage, of the Calculating Machine, I saw once at a Conversazione of the Graphic Club, held at the London University. I thought he looked like a man to be always at war with the Italian organists. Sloman, a Jew composer, and a popular singer, I have heard and talked with at Evans' in Covent-Garden, like the "Cider Cel-

155

lars" a rare place for drink and song in late hours after the theatres.   Very late out of Evans' it was a sight to watch the country waggons coming in with vegetables to the early market: a sight worth waiting for.   Cobden and O'Connell I have heard at the Corn Law League in Covent-Garden Theatre. There was no chance of hearing them in the Borough of Finsbury, where they would have been met by the chartist cry of "Manhood Suffrage and political freedom even before cheap bread!"   Foresti, Silvio Pellico's fellow-prisoner at Spielberg, after his release, wrote to me from America.   They said that his first inquiry on coming out of Spielberg was concerning Mazzini.   Frances Wright (Madame d'Arusmont), the author of *A Few Days at Athens*, one of Owen's New Harmony people, a rather handsome woman who had the look of being six feet high, I heard lecture on her return from America, and I occasionally met her.   Robert Owen, too, I would sometimes meet.   There was no magnetic influence from him, a man of one idea, unpoetic, without a spark of imagination, very wearisome in his singular capacity for reiteration.

Landor I never saw, though I had many friendly letters from him, contributions also to my *English Republic*, and to *Pen and Pencil*, a weekly illustrated newspaper which had a brief existence of a few weeks under my editing and art management, in 1854 or 1855.   When, resolute not to pay the damages cast against him in a trial for libel, a libel which the quick-tempered old poet ought not to have uttered, although indeed it was not uncalled for, Landor sold off all he had and quitted England to end his days in Italy, he left in my hands a pile of leaflets to be distributed in justification of his action. It was really a repetition of the libel, and, thinking such a course unworthy of so great a man, I burned the leaflets, every one. Somewhile after he sent to Browning, as a present for me, a large picture he supposed to be by Michael Angelo. Landor at one time had a large collection of pictures, supposed to be genuine, but seldom if ever of any worth. This "Angelo" might be of that sort. I called on Browning (the only time I ever saw him) to look at and to speak about the picture. It was a "Last Judgment," a poor and very unpleasant composition, too large and too unpleasant to be hung in a private house, a gift as of a white elephant, neither to be accepted nor refused. I got out of the difficulty by Browning telling me that the old man had no right to give it, as all his "belongings" really belonged to his brother, Robert Landor, on whom Walter Savage was living. So Browning took charge of the elephant and relieved me.

Richard Oastler I once met in Hetherington's shop; a tall, burly, Yorkshire man, with strangely protruding eyes, a stout Tory, but stronger as a factory-reformer. Rowland Hill, to whom we owe the penny postage, I spoke with once, on some newspaper business. With Sir Joseph Paxton, of the

Crystal Palace, who had been the Duke of Devonshire's head-gardener at Chatsworth, I once also had an interview. It was to obtain his interest and help for, I believe, *Pen and Pencil*. He received me courteously, but could afford me at most a few minutes, pointing to the clock on the chimney-piece against which he stood; then detained me nearly an hour to tell me of his heavy losses on the *Daily News* and the useless expense of Dickens' editorship of that paper. Francis Place, the Westminster tailor who returned two members to Parliament, for he was a power in Westminster, and Sir Francis Burdett and John Cam Hobhouse both owed their election to his influence, a fierce Malthusian with a large family, was an old man when I knew him. I used to consult him when I wanted advice as to getting up a public meeting. Colonel Perronet Thompson was the first public speaker I ever heard, it was at a Polish meeting. I came to know him in the Peoples' International League. It was only in quite his later days that he was made a General. His radical principles stood in his way, though he had been Governor of Sierra Leone. I have understood that he had expended more than £30,000 in advocacy of liberal measures. As proprietor and editor of the *Westminster Review* in its best days, he was one of the earliest and most important promoters of the agitation against the Corn Laws. I recollect, as far back as in the time of my apprenticeship, a cut in the *Westminster Review* in sharp illustration of the effect of those laws, drawn by Thomas Landseer and engraved by Bonner, a cut of a cage of monkeys, every monkey struggling to get his neighbour's food from the trough in front of them. A widely accomplished man was the Colonel; his five volumes of *Political Exercises* (which he gave me), mainly reprints from the *Review*, are among the best of political writings that I know. P. A. Taylor, with whom also I was acquainted, the father of the Member of Parliament, of the firm of Courtauld, Taylor, & Courtauld, silk-manufacturers, was also one of the first Anti-Corn-Law men. Thompson, Taylor, and W. E. Hickson (who succeeded Thompson as proprietor of the *Westminster*), with Ebenezer Elliott, the " Corn-Law Rhymer," deserve to rank in that movement as precursors and preparers of the way of Bright and Cobden.

For George Dawson, the popular lecturer and preacher, I wrote a series of leaders in his newspaper, the *Birmingham Journal*. A fluent and good orator, though not great, I used to think his manner had been too much affected by his early education as show-boy at prize-exhibitions of his father's school. He was not an original thinker, but did very good work in popularising Carlyle, and in general politics, always frankly at the public service, with or without pay. Another good man on the popular side was Francis William Newman, the brother of the Cardinal, not a man of the same high genius, but a man of culture and fine thought, with excellent sympathies and intentions, but, as it seemed to me, hesitating in action and always appearing to doubt if his accepted course had been really right in politics. He, I used to think, ought to have stooped under the yoke of the Roman Church, and John Henry to have stood upright as a leader of progress, which he might have been. Good also, and always prompt on the public ground, was Dr. John Epps, a homœopathic physician, whose father, having made a fortune by what the French call *charcuterie*, sent his eldest son John to College. We spoke laughingly, not, however, with disrespect, of him as the " Homœopathic Napoleon," his stature and figure and accustomed posture reminding one of the " Little Corporal." He was a ready, if not an eloquent speaker, too often mixing the hygienic with the political, a plain, sound teacher whose heart was in his speech, a good and sincere liberal. Dr. Bowring was another man to be depended on in any proceedings toward reform. I saw him often on public questions, once breakfasted with him at his house in Queen Square, Westminster, and had pleasant meeting with him, after his return from China. There was a little of the Girondist, of the pedagogue about him, and I have no faith in his too facile translations ; but he was a good citizen and a man to be respected.

I had not the same respect for Charles Dickens. For all his genius as a novelist, I have always thought that his real vocation was as an actor of low comedy, much as the world might have lost by such a change. Warm-hearted and sentimental, but not unselfish, he was not the gentleman. There was no grace of manner, no soul of nobility in him. When he and Wilkie Collins and Wills (the editor of *Household Words*) went out, taking Dickens' doctor with them, to eat " the most expensive dinner they could get," it was an action that marked the Amphytrion of the feast, if not the others also. It is an unpleasant anecdote, but it was told me by the doctor himself, who had to prescribe for all three next day. The doctor's fees of course would be reckoned as part of the expensiveness of the dinner. Other things I knew of Dickens make me rate him as far inferior as a man (indeed I would also place him as a writer) to Thackeray. I knew two of Dickens' uncles, both named Barrow: the one a draftsman on wood, who did much work for me, the other, who had been in India, a literary man and editor of an unsuccessful paper, the *Mirror of Parliament*, projected and provided for by Spottiswood, the Queen's Printer. Spottiswood was also proprietor of the *Pictorial Times*, an opposition to the *Illustrated London News*, and Barrow introduced me to him, as he wanted some change and improvement in the paper. I was offered a partnership as artistic editor, but had to decline the offer, as I did not feel that under the proposed agreement I should be free in my department. Not long afterwards I heard that the paper had been given up after a loss of £10,000. The copyright was bought by Ingram for £100.

M

Of two men with whom I had relations, George Jacob Holyoake and Charles Bradlaugh, I must now speak, that I may not be thought afraid to do so: not afraid, but indeed unwilling so far as concerns Holyoake, with whom for some years I had close connection. He began his public life by a foolish provocation of prosecution for blasphemy, thereby gaining such credit and notoriety as might be due to the "Last Martyr for Atheism." With such object in view, the martyrdom was of small account; but, taken as only the rash impulsiveness of an over-earnest young man, it gave him admittance to the ranks of lovers of free thought. So welcomed and made much of, he worked himself up to be the leader of a party, the party of those who considered free-thought and disbelief to be synonymous terms, who may indeed be likened to the bird which, escaping from its cage, perches on the next tree, not knowing how nor caring to attempt a farther flight, and whose monotonous song is merely the contented inane reiteration of "I am free." Looking back upon Holyoake's work, I can give no better account of it so far as free thought was concerned. But independently of that, he had place among us for his adhesion to the principles of the Charter, and for some aidance in the coöperative endeavours of the time: not by any means of the importance which he now claims for himself. And he was liked as a kindly-natured, amiable man. So he made his way, a poor speaker, though not wanting words, not so much leading or swaying an audience as expressing what it desired to hear, and therefore popular, — the mouthpiece of a party that only wanted to be encouraged on its predetermined road. Looking back, I find in his writing in his paper — the *Reasoner* — little of original thought or sound reasoning. Half-educated and weak, he never grew. Yet after a time he was dissatisfied. Staying in my house at Miteside for some days, seeing his state of doubtfulness, I counseled him to make his condition of health an excuse for discontinuing the *Reasoner* for a few weeks, to give him time to seriously sift his own mind. "If," I said, "you find yourself still convinced of the righteousness and usefulness of your course, you have sufficient hold on your followers to resume work, all the better for your rest; if, on the other hand, you find your path is really tending nowhere, be brave enough to abandon it, and apply your future differently!" He did not follow my advice, but long afterwards said that he wished he had.

In fact, he was getting weary of the poor reiteration of Atheism, the word standing between him and friends who could not recognise him openly under such a garment. So at last he doffed the unseemliness and put on what seemed the more respectable garb of "Secularism," rather a vague term which did not too exactly describe his still-continued nibblings at religious theories and wranglings upon theological formulas. I began to find him inconsistent and slippery; and when, as it seemed to me, he was also false to the popular cause, and only self-seeking, I parted from him, not without harsh words which even now, rereading them, I can not honestly call back or soften.

Bradlaugh was a very different man. Sturdy and conscientious, meaning all he said, and never afraid to say what he meant. I had little sympathy with his irreligious opinions, nor do I know that there was more than occasional agreement between us on political grounds. But I had never any reason to do other than respect him. I take it that sheer want of the imaginative faculty was at the base of his theory of disbelief. It was not in his nature to believe, certainly not in the supernatural. But it was in his nature to take an active part in what lay around him, and to stoutly contend against whatever he thought wrong in theory or practice; and he was true to his nature, whether as iconoclast or reformer. There seemed an indication of something else in his affection for the companion of his early days, James Thomson, the poet (true poet) of the *City of Dreadful Night,* and in Thomson's affection for him. Certainly it should be said that this indefatigable iconoclast was a kindly-natured man, as one may be even if a born fighter. And he was a man who made the best of himself; to whom, I would say, self-culture, if only to train him for the fight (and who shall dare even so to narrow his motives?) was felt as a duty. Unlike the man of whom I have just spoken, there was growth in him. I had not heard him for years when, being in England, I was asked by an American friend to take him to hear a lecture by Bradlaugh. We went, were much pleased with the lecturer, and for myself, I was surprised at a notable improvement in both oratory and manner. Had he lived, I believe he would have made a distinguished record as Member of Parliament, — courageous, persistent, indomitable, and of strict integrity. So I judge him, differing *toto cœlo* from him on the ground of life and action.

CHAPTER XXI

Ruskin; John Forster; Robson; Derwent Coleridge; Wordsworth; Dr. Davy; Harriet Martineau; Mrs. Millner Gibson; Mediums; Dupotet; Kossuth; Medici; Ronge; The Hills; Mrs. Craik; Dobell; Rossetti; Swinburne; Barmby; Thom; The Chartist Epic; Robert Montgomery; Lover; G. S. Phillips; Hughes; Mayne Reid.

I CAN keep no sort of order in these reminiscences. Ruskin I saw but once, then by appointment in the shop of Ellis, the bookseller, in King Street, Covent-Garden: a very pleasant meeting. The purchase of Brantwood was pleasantly arranged in a couple of letters. But I knew of him not only through my admiration for his writings (admiring him as The Poet, beyond all verse-makers of his time, and for the keen political insight of his at first so much mis-understood book, *Unto This Last*), but farther as a man of the noblest nature. I knew from W. B. Scott, very friendly with him until differing views of artistic teaching (at the Workingmen's College and elsewhere) sundered them, of his great life and gen-erosities. Scott, no doubt, was right on the Art question. Forster of the *Examiner*, whom Thornton Hunt labeled as the "Beadle of the Universe" on account of his pomposity, I met only at a conversa-zione; but I wrote occasionally in the *Examiner*; on one occasion a whole page of review with translations of Victor Hugo's *Châtiments*, for which my only *honorarium* was a note of admiration from Landor, and Hugo's photograph sent to me by the great Frenchman. Of Forster's *Life of Sir John Eliot* I possess a copy given me by my friend John Robson, the printer of the book, a printer not only excellent in his own art, but a man of various accomplishments, a Greek and Latin scholar, not unacquainted with Hebrew, and a collaborator with Dyce in the preparation of Dyce's edition of Shakspere. With the Rev. Derwent Coleridge, the brother of Hartley, I once spent a delightful day at Keswick and walking over Blencathra (Saddleback, from its form), the nearest mountain to Skiddaw. He appeared to me a sensible, well-informed, genial, and liberal clergyman, hardly deserving to be girded at by Carlyle because he was too wise a man not to get on better in the world than his brother or his father. But the getting on in the world was itself the offence to Carlyle. (Duffy's *Conversations*, p. 60.) Wordsworth, though I lived in the Lake Country, I never saw. Miteside was far away from Rydale across the mountains, and he died in 1850, before I had come within his reach from Brantwood. Perhaps I had not cared to visit him, not sure how he might receive the Chartist and Republican, for I could not forget what I had been told by Margaret Gillies, the miniature-painter, who was staying at Rydale to take Wordsworth's portrait when the news came of Frost's reprieve : that the old Northman stamped his foot with vexation and rage.

Professor Wilson was much oftener talked of than Wordsworth, and was evidently much more in the hearts and remembrance of the Lake folk. So, indeed, was poor Hartley Coleridge. They were before my time, as certainly was Sir Humphrey Davy; but I dined once at the Swan at Grasmere, in company with my good Coniston doctor, Mr. Gibson, with Sir Humphrey's brother, Dr. Davy, at a doctors' dinner.

At Brantwood I was near enough to Ambleside to visit Harriet Martineau, and to be visited by her. Plain and, judging from her portraits, far from prepossessing in her young days, she had become with age a good-looking, comely, interesting old lady, very deaf, but cheerful and eager for news, which she did not always catch correctly. With all her manly self-dependence and strict intentional honesty, with all her credit for practical common sense, she was as much a poet at heart as her brother, the Rev. James; a romancer even in the region of economical facts, even in those hard *Poor Law Tales*, when under Lord Brougham she was preparing to prove the necessity for the Poor Law Amendment Act, that crowning harshness of Whig rule. She has never had justice done to her on this ground of romance. It matters little: if she did find Cumberland cheeses so hard that they struck fire as they rolled down the rocks, and the peasant girls indulging in an excess of jewelry, we are still justified in esteeming her as a true and brave woman. Another grand woman I had the honour of knowing was Mrs. Millner Gibson, a staunch Liberal, her house a centre and place of *rendezvous* for Liberals, a firm friend of Mazzini and Italian freedom. She, too, like Harriet Martineau, had her weak spot of credence for some things not " dreamed of in your philosophy." At the next house to hers, that of Dr. Ashburner, by Hyde Park Corner, I was with her at a reception given to that chief of humbugs, the American medium, Foster. Various were his tricks, but none convincing to the unprepared. Going from the exhibition-room into another, I there saw Mrs. Gibson, Sir Emerson Tennant, and a third person, watching a round table that, with its legs in the air, was expected to lift itself and turn over to a normal position. I did not wait to see the accomplishment. Another fraud even more transparent than Foster was a Mrs. Marshall, a rather low-lived medium and table-rapper, who allowed you to look under the table because there was " nothing but wacancy there." She gave me messages from a dead (never-living) brother, whose name I led to ; and was plainly disposed to be fooled by or to fool her visitors to the top of their bent. Once, many years before, I had been present at a *séance* given by the French magnetist, the Baron Dupotet, when the power of magnetic passes was fairly exhibited on two young girls, Dupotet's patients. Unless my recollection deceives me, there were present Mrs. Trollope and a deaf son, his deafness apparently lost while under the magnetic influence.

Kossuth's oratory I never heard, but with my friend Worcell I spent some hours with him one morning, and was pleased with his suavity and bright conversation. Medici, a tall, handsome, soldierly-looking man, one of the heroes of the defence of Rome, afterwards under Victor Emmanuel Governor of Sicily, I had met at an evening reception in London. Thiers, a mean old clothes-man in appearance, passed me once at the entrance of the Chamber of Deputies in Paris, followed immediately by General Cavaignac. I could not repress a wish that the tall, grim soldier would pick up the historic liar and fling the noisome thing to the ground. Not even for Louis Napoleon have I felt more abhorrence than for Thiers, the woman-massacrer in those sadly mistaken days of the Commune. Johannes Ronge, a sort of mild Luther, I knew slightly. He spent some time at the house of my friend Scott in Newcastle; and sorely grieved the heart of Mrs. Scott's mother, as the old lady herself told me, by his excessive addiction to cold water, hanging out his wet sheets of a morning to dry on the rail at the stair-top. A worthy enough man, well meaning, but with far too high an opinion of his own importance in the world's work. His wife appeared to be a sensible and estimable woman. She kept at one time a kindergarten in London. Mrs. Hill, a daughter of Dr. Southwood Smith, the wife of the editor of an extreme free-thought paper at Wisbeach, the *Star in the East*, I knew well; and knew also, when they were children, her five daughters, five or six. One of them was Octavia Hill, since prominent in good work. Another married a son of G. H. Lewes.

With Dinah Muloch, afterwards Mrs. Craik, I was also well acquainted, an over-tall and in younger days somewhat spindly woman, not beautiful, but good, the goodness flavouring all her writings. At her house at Hampstead I met Sidney Dobell, a pleasant, gentlemanly young fellow, the author of *Balder*. Once at Dante Rossetti's rooms in Chatham Place, by Blackfriar's Bridge, I think in 1861, I met Swinburne, then a young man, but looking like a boy, and with a boyish manner, jumping about as he became excited in speaking, yet interesting and attractive. For Rossetti I had great regard, though I saw not much of him. He seemed to me to be rather an Italian than an Englishman; an Italian of the time of the Medici, not without thoughts and superstitions of that period, a man of genius both in art and literature; one, however, hindering the other, the literary preponderating, and by which he will be best recollected. His poems will surely last; and there are no finer translations extant than his from the Italian, of "*Dante and his Circle.*" I find him fully and fairly noticed in the *Autobiographical Notes* of W. B. Scott; so fully that I need not attempt addition to his record. Powerful, subtle, and highly imaginative, Rossetti's poems are the very antithesis of those of Charles Mackay, whom I knew, of Eliza Cook, whom I never met, or of Martin Farquhar Tupper, to

whom I was introduced at the opening of Mudie's
Lending Library, and whom I might have passed as
a most respectable grocer and possible churchwarden.
More poetic than Tupper, not only in appearance,
was Goodwyn Barmby, who in his callow days was
a very earnest itinerant all-on-his-own-hook preacher
of a sort of socialism; but who, after much well-borne
buffeting, settled down as a quiet and respectable
Unitarian minister at Pontefact, in Yorkshire, where
he married for his second wife the daughter of the
Governor of the Gaol.   We were always friendly, and
he came across the country to visit me at Brantwood,
and to show how little he had changed except in
outer clerical appearance.   He offered me the use of
his pulpit; but I never had the opportunity of accepting his offer.   Truly a poet, albeit in a small
Burns-diluted way, was poor Willie Thom, an Inver-
urie weaver, a little man with a club-foot, who was
seduced to come on a poetic pilgrimage to London,
somewhere about 1844, meeting there at first with
much congratulation, public dinners, pattings on the
back, and kindness, from Dickens, the Howitts, Fox,
Eliza Cook, and others, but with no success in his search
for literary employment, for which indeed he had little
capacity.   That a poor untaught weaver should have
written so well, was his sole recommendation.   An
amiable, weak man, he met with much personal
favour; but what could be done with him or for him?
Disappointed, with the help of Fox, who was a good
friend to him, and at whose house I first met him, he

returned to Scotland to die outside of the gates of Fame. Friendly patronage could do no more.

Such ineffectual fostering brings before me the name of Capel Lofft, the patron of Kirke White! A nephew of Lofft, of the same name (I believe he was a barrister in Gray's Inn), wrote and printed an "epic" poem. The poem being "Chartist," I suppose was the occasion of my hearing of it, and I asked for and obtained a copy. It was a strange jumble of blank, very blank, verse and rhyme: the speeches being rhyme, the descriptive portions in unrhymed lengths. The story was of an imaginary attempt at revolution in England, headed by one "Ernest," a young enthusiast whose part was that of "King Arthur come again," and who, winning one battle against the opponent nobles, in the moment of victory disappears, Arthur like, when the successful rebels would proclaim him king: the whole story reading like a romance of the German "Peasants' War," with a more fortunate but most unlikely result. Hardly had the book appeared, and been noticed not unfavourably by the *Quarterly Review*, when the author, fearing it was too potent an incitement to rebellion, called in all the copies and withdrew from the notoriety he had begun to provoke. Fox, unable to get a copy, asked to borrow mine. When I handed it to him he remarked, " Do not expect to have this back again ! I have lost so many books by lending, that now I never think of returning those I borrow. I lent some volumes to Southwood Smith.

He never returned them, but one day when I was dining with him, he pointed them out to me in his library,
and bade me notice how well he had had them bound."
Of course, so warned, I had my book back in due time.
I have never seen another copy.   It is one of the
curiosities of literature.

The Rev. Robert Montgomery, the author of *Satan*,
once consulted me concerning the illustrating of
another of his great poems, *Woman*.   He was a
handsome and popular clergyman, full of words, but
his poetic gift perhaps fairly to be estimated from
some lines in *The Real Devil's Walk*, a rather lengthy
imitation of Coleridge's.   Montgomery meets the Devil
in Piccadilly; and they pass without greeting, for

> "Montgomery knew nothing of Satan,
> Though Satan knew Montgomery."

Lover, a poorer Moore, not so prolific, but perhaps
more genuine, I once heard sing one of his songs —
" What would you do ? Love ! " to his own accompani-
ment.   He struck me only as a pleasant little man of
society, of not much weight.   Not at all a man of society
was G. S. Phillips, with whom I spent some hours in
Huddersfield, where he was Secretary to a Mechanics'
Institute.   I knew him from his writing some fresh and
brightly clever articles on Sherwood Forest in Lees'
Present Age, in which he wrote over the pseudonym
of " January Searle."   He was a tall, good-looking,
earnest, or rather impulsive man, who would, I
should think, make friends quickly and perhaps not

keep them. Scott, hearing something of him, wrote to invite him to Newcastle. He meaned to take him to some philosophical meeting; but the appointed evening arrived, and no Phillips. Too late for the meeting came a brief note to say that he, Phillips, had found a pleasant fellow-traveler on the train, and they two were enjoying themselves at the Turk's Head, or other Newcastle hotel, and would Scott join them there? I knew no more of him till he called upon me in New York. I did not care to keep up the acquaintance. He had taken to drink, and the last I heard of him was of his being in an asylum. Hughes, the author of *Tom Brown's Schooldays*, I used to see while engraving Richard Doyle's designs for *Scouring the White Horse*, for Macmillan. Mayne Reid I met once at the office of the *Illustrated London News*.

CHAPTER XXII

Millais and other Artists; The Foggos; Wornum; Sibson; Tom Landseer; George Cruikshank; Tennyson; Orsini; Kiallmark; Richard Lane; Flatou; Garth Wilkinson; Gilchrist; Linnell; Sykes.

To continue the catalogue of names of those whom I have known, more or less, before I left London for the North, or while I was living in the North, or at a time of some few years when I was seeking to establish myself again in London, I may add to the list already given of artist acquaintances or friends — Millais, whom I recollect as a young Apollo, supremely handsome; Whistler, always eccentric; Boughton; Madox Brown; Munro, Durham, and Patric Park, three sculptors; E. M. Ward, and his wife, also a painter and not inferior to her husband (she was the daughter of G. R. Ward, the mezzotint engraver); the two brothers Foggo, George and James, two gaunt Scotchmen, painters of large unsuccessful historical figure subjects, long since gone out of sight. One of the brothers, I forget which, had a habit of twitching or wriggling his nose, a habit also noticeable in another gaunt Scotchman, Lord Brougham. It was said that this Foggo and his lordship were once opponent speakers at a public meeting, and the noses of the two men, alike in general personal appearance, wagged against each other, to the great amusement of the beholders. I only knew the Foggos, worthy men, I believe, if not successful painters, as rather captious members of the Institute of Fine Arts, at which we were often in collision. Wornum, Scott's and Sibson's friend, I also knew there. For a meeting of the Institute in the Rooms of the Society of Arts, Wornum had prepared a lecture on "Roman Coins"; but when the hour came was too modest or wanting in self-confidence to deliver it. As a member of the Council, it fell to me to deliver it for him. At another similar meeting I read a paper on Thomas Sibson, then recently dead, a paper partly my own, partly by Scott, and I then exhibited his designs for the *History of England*, the only time they have been seen in public.

Tom Landseer, the engraver, I recollect as a short, broad-shouldered, deaf man, the eldest, and, to my thinking, the most talented of the three Landseer brothers, his *Monkeyana*, or "Men in Miniature," only etchings as they were, and his other etchings of animals, evincing more originality and vigour of drawing than is to be seen in the excellently painted pictures of the more famous Sir Edwin, the Sir Thomas Lawrence of animal life.

George Cruikshank was a well-built, good-looking, good-natured, impulsive man, a bluff speaker who could call a spade a spade. I had had a dispute with a publisher as to my charge for engraving one

N

of Cruikshank's drawings, and it was thought that I might be influenced by a remark that Mr. Cruikshank deemed my price too high. I replied that it was no business of his; but the next time I saw him I asked him why he had so interfered. "My dear Linton," was his answer, "the publisher is a liar." Once at the Artists' Annuity Fund, a society to which we both belonged, a meeting was held to consider the expulsion of a defaulting officer. In the midst of a discussion as to whether the defaulter should be prosecuted, Cruikshank entered the room. He had heard nothing of what had passed, but when he caught the drift of the argument, his pity for the delinquent, a man we had all liked as well as trusted, led him to protest against the intended action. "We must not be hard on the poor man, and as to thinking him without means of defence, how did we know he was not supplied with our own moneys?" The general laugh did not disconcert him. It was as innocently uttered as the comment of the man at the Tichbourne trial — "He didn't care whether he was Sir Roger or not, but he could not bear to see a poor man robbed of his rights." In his later years Cruikshank was a rigid teetotaler, devoting his artistic power to the advocacy of temperance. It was not unfairly said that it was time for him to abstain, as he certainly had enjoyed a full man's share of drink.

During my ownership of Brantwood, but while I was resident in London, Tennyson was for a summer at Coniston, with his family occupying "Tent Lodge," near the Waterhead, the house in which usually lived the Misses Romney. Tennyson was reported to have had a cross chalked on the gate, that he might not miss it at night under the dark tree-shadows. While I was living at Brantwood, a visit to Joseph Cowen at Blaydon made me acquainted with Orsini, at Cowen's, after his escape from an Austrian prison. A fine-looking man, handsome, energetic, and pleasant in manner, I heard him lecture on Italy at the Blaydon Mechanics' Institute, and saw him again at my temporary lodging in London. He called on me there to take leave, with one Dr. Bernard, a French socialist, whom I knew to be an extremist. I seemed to forebode some unlucky adventure, little however supposing what were his intentions. I take it, that his plan of action was motived not by any care not to endanger himself, but by a propensity to cleverness. A brave man, thoroughly in earnest, he was not above a certain hankering for applause. Returned to London, I had pleasant intimacy with the Kiallmarks, near neighbours : Mr. Kiallmark, a most amiable man, an accomplished musician and improvisatore on the piano, the son of a Danish composer. I was also on friendly terms with the family of Richard Lane, the brother of Edward Lane, the Egyptologist. Richard Lane was an excellent etcher, and known also for his lithographic portraits from the painting of Sir Thomas Lawrence. The eldest of Lane's three fair daughters, a charming woman, was a first-rate flower-painter, her talent perhaps inherited from Gainsborough, to whom, either on the father's or the mother's side, she was related. Woolner I once saw, in his studio. Dining with Alexander Johnston, a painter after the fashion of Wilkie, I met a picture dealer named Flatou, who to his knowledge of pictures added a rare faculty of mimicry, and who was also a ventriloquist. He entertained us at dinner with admirable specimens of various English dialects, and afterwards, taking his seat in the next room, gave a conversation between two lovers from *Fra Diavolo*, a piece then being acted at Fechter's Theatre, imitating Fechter's peculiar accent; and on coming into the drawing-room amused us with ventriloquism. He had the wisdom, or it may have been from real love of Art, to insist on having the oil sketches of pictures he bought, and the sketches he kept for himself, a beautiful collection in his own house. It was told of him, that one day going into the country for a first view of some artist's pictures, he telegraphed for a carriage to take him to the artist's house at some distance from the station. At the station he found that a rival dealer already occupied the only conveyance, and refused to give up his place. So they drove together to the artist's house, where Flatou was first to alight, sending in his card as " Mr. Flatou and friend." The friend did not get sight of the pictures till Flatou had made his way.

I have visited at the house of Marston, the playwright, the father of Philip Bourke Marston, the blind poet; and at that of De Morgan, the actuary, whose wife was a spiritualist, and had a craze of stones being thrown at her by the spirits as she passed a certain house. Dr. Garth Wilkinson, the amiable physician, I knew well. A Swedenborgian, he too had a touch of the spiritualist malady, which brought out a volume of inspired poems, outside the ordinary laws of poetic form. I had to thank him for an introduction to Emerson, who, when in England, had been attracted by him. With Gilchrist I worked on his *Life of Blake*, having to get up the illustrations. So one Sunday I went with Gilchrist to see Linnell at his house near Red Hill. The old man gave us dinner in a large, barely-furnished room at a long deal table — deal or oak, at which he and his wife and daughter and two of his three sons sat down at irregular intervals of time and place; and after dinner we were shown his Blake treasures, his portrait of Blake, the original drawings for the *Book of Job*, proof impressions of the plates, and Blake's designs for Dante, — taking care not to leave us alone with any. The Dante designs, some mere scrawls, some highly finished and coloured, were drawn in a large book, which Linnell had given to Blake that he might make use of it in his last sickness, during which Linnell had provided for him. It had the look of a speculation, a purpose of being repaid for services to the poor friend; but it did not appear that Linnell had ever attempted to make a profit of them, but kept them as valued mementos only. A strange, dry, withered old man was the painter, quaint in speech, with strange utterance of strange opinions, a man who might have admired Blake as much for his literary incoherences as for his artistic imagination. Beginning life as a picture cleaner and repairer, he had risen to be a great painter and fairly successful. He had built himself a house on a high ridge of the Surrey country, overlooking an extensive weald. The site was so commanding that some one suggested (it was during talk of a French invasion) that the house would certainly be taken as the headquarters of the French General. "They can't do it, sir!" very positively answered Linnell, "they can't do it! it's against the law."

One man very worthy of love and admiration whom I came to know in these later London days was Godfrey Sykes, Alfred Stevens' favourite pupil at Sheffield, the best of the artists employed at South Kensington Museum and School of Art, highly esteemed there, but starved on a low salary until, his health failing, the fear of losing him aroused a wiser and more careful generosity. It was too late to save him from dying of consumption. A man of genius, bright, witty, delicately handsome, and of most affectionate nature, it was a pleasure, not unmixed with the sadness of anxious fear, to know him for a few, too few years. In his art he had followed worthily in the steps of "the master," as Stevens was always lovingly styled by him.

CHAPTER XXIII

Alfred Stevens; Young Mitchell; Wehnert; The Wellington Monument.

ALFRED STEVENS, the designer and maker of the Monument to the Duke of Wellington in St. Paul's Cathedral, was my very dear friend. Born at Blandford in Dorsetshire in 1817, his father a decorative and heraldic painter, he almost before he had passed from childhood displayed a passionate love and more than aptitude for Art; and that fortunately recognised by a neighbouring clergyman, the Hon. and Rev. Samuel Best, he was through that gentleman's interest sent at the age of sixteen to travel and educate himself in Italy. There he remained, studying incessantly, for nine years, somewhile at Naples, sometimes at Florence, copying frescoes in the churches and convents, so many that he would say he thought he had copied everything; then copying Titian's pictures; then working for Thorwaldsen, who had a great regard for him. Returning to England in 1842, his first employment was as one of the masters in the Government School of Design at Somerset House, a position he held efficiently for four years, during that time also making his magnificent design for the doorway of the Jermyn Street

School of Mines, a design worthy of comparison with the celebrated gates of Ghiberti. Later on, in 1848 or '49, he went to Sheffield as designer to the iron works of Messrs. Hoole & Robson. While there he greatly assisted, if only with advice, his friend, Mr. Young Mitchell in the School of Design. Godfrey Sykes, John Gamble, Reuben Townroe, learned of him there, all afterwards holding positions at South Kensington, all looking to him as their master. Not that Young Mitchell was inefficient; but the higher influence was also appreciated. Mitchell, with whom I had been allied in the Institute of Fine Arts, before he had the appointment to Sheffield, had introduced me to Stevens, and before I went northward we had become close friends. He would come and sit beside me when in after hours I sat engraving in one of my work-rooms at 85 Hatton-Garden. He was back again in London, after rather less than three years in Sheffield, and I was often with him during occasional visits to the South.

In 1855 I came back to live in London, and after that I saw more of him. Myself and Edward Wehnert (the water-colour painter) were, I think, his closest friends; we, with Elmore and Penrose, almost his only visitors at the house on Haverstock Hill, rising toward Hampstead, where he was preparing for his great work on the Monument and also for Mr. Holford's commission for a chimney-piece in Dorchester House, Holford's mansion in Park Lane. Not only the chimney-piece (which alone Stevens lived to execute), but the whole room and its furniture were to have been of Stevens' design. Engrossed with his work, he never went into society. It was difficult to drag him out even to dine with his friend Wehnert's family, a brother and three sisters all fond of him; and having called on him with Wehnert to take him to dinner, I have known him turn back, when as the door was opened he saw an extra hat in the hall, with, " O Wehnert! I forgot," —that there was something to prevent his stay; and we had almost to force him in. Not that he was averse to or unfit for conversation; it was only the shyness of a man who did not care to make new friends. Incessantly at his work, I have gone in upon him at ten o'clock in the morning: " What, breakfasting so late as this? Stevens!" " My dear fellow, I breakfasted at four o'clock." He would come in to dinner in the next house, a house in which he lived, adjoining his studio and opening from it; and before the dinner was placed on the table would be carving on a book-case or the edge of a sideboard. The only relaxation he took was a few days' voyage in a west country friend's yacht, the sea greatly enjoyed by him. A day at South Kensington with him and Sykes and Wehnert, to see the Raffaele Cartoons, removed there from the obscurity of Hampton Court to a sufficient light, is one of my pleasantest remembrances. The Hogarths were the only pictures we cared to look at afterwards. Another pleasant day was when we went together to see the boat-race, and after seeing it walked through acres (it seemed miles) of wall-flowers from Barnes to Richmond, where we dined, coming back to Haverstock Hill in the late evening. Many happy times at his house, at my own, at the Wehnerts', and at the house of Sykes, should also have place among my recollections. Not a great, but a good talker, with much to talk of, — Italy and Art, — he was a desirable companion. And beyond all delight of companionship was the appreciation of his greatness as an artist and the simple worth of the man.

Putting out of question the special excellences of our few great men, he stands forth as the most thoroughly accomplished artist we have ever had in England. As a sculptor, with a knowledge also of architecture and of the sculptor's relation to that, we have no one to equal him. As a painter, good in drawing, in composition, and in colour, he did enough to show that he would have taken a highest place, had his attention been more confined to that. His few portraits were fine. His designs for iron-work and pottery, and of general decoration, had a wide range and were of remarkable excellence His motto, — " I know but of one art," — a motto borrowed from Michael Angelo, characterised his whole work, in which, for all its variety, there was nothing careless or inferior or unworthy of his powers. He was so thoroughly conscientious in his art, so thoroughly conscious, too, of what was good, that though a sure and rapid worker, he was not easily satisfied. This almost fastidiousness prevented a business-like punctuality in the performance of his commissions, and was the cause of considerable friction with his employers on the Monument, the Commissioners of the Board of Works, the governmental money-providers. So he was worried by delay in payments; and when from too close application to work his health gave way, the worry became greater. It helped indeed to kill him. Other annoyances he had in the poor place given in the Cathedral to the Monument, and in the absurd objection of Dean Millman (the legal custodian of the Cathedral) to the completion of the Monument as originally designed with an equestrian statue of the Duke at the top. From a slight attack of paralysis in 1873 he recovered sufficiently to bring his work virtually to completion; but on the 30th of April, 1875, an attack of apoplexy stayed the artist's hand.

In person Stevens was rather below the average height, squarely built, showing considerable strength; once remarkably proved in Sheffield, where, attacked from behind by a garrotter, he stooped and flung the fellow over his head, only shaking himself as a dog might when, a few minutes later, he entered a friend's house and quietly told of the transaction. His head was large, his face, while I knew him, clean-shaved, his features were expressive, he had keen eyes, a sensitive mouth, and a general look of cheerful calm strength and goodness. He was neat in his person for all the usual carelessness of an artist, and in his dress looking like and often taken for a Catholic priest. Gentle in his heart and in his demeanour, and, though conscious of his own ability, in no way self-assertive, he was a man to be both loved and admired. It is something to know that, however undervalued in his life, his reputation has been steadily growing since his death.

CHAPTER XXIV

Garibaldi in Sicily; The British Legion; Captain de Rohan.

In 1860, when Garibaldi was gone upon his Sicilian expedition (planned by Mazzini, and successfully begun by Rosalino Pilo, who fell in the moment of victory as Garibaldi landed to pursue the work), word came to friends of Italy in England that it were well if we could send out an English contingent, to give help and to prove our sympathy. A Committee, of which I was a member, was quickly formed, and measures were promptly taken to enrol volunteers for what was called an Excursion to Sicily, so called to keep clear of proved illegality, and so not to compel the interference of the Government. We were not interfered with, and soon had a gathering, a gathering of a strange crowd, earnest men, men with selfish ends, men of good repute and not so good, the sort of mixture in all such enterprises. Our work was mainly forwarded by a staunch Mazzinian, Captain De Rohan, a native of Jersey, who had made his mark in South America fighting for Peruvian independence, and who, like Garibaldi and so many of the Italian patriots, had returned to Europe for the cause of Italy. De Rohan had already from his own means chartered the three steamships which took Garibaldi's force to Sicily; the "Washington," the "Franklin," and the "Oregon." He helped us in the purchase of arms and organising, with advice and money, and as friend and agent of Garibaldi took general charge of the Expedition. In twenty-three days we had enrolled and were ready to despatch a thousand men, armed and equipped. I went with the main body of them by a night train to Harwich, where a steamer was provided to carry them to Sicily. The first action on reaching Harwich was to hold a court-martial on one of the officers, a "Major" Hicks, of whom we had received most unsatisfactory accounts. He was dismissed, and in an altercation forcibly ejected from De Rohan's room by an American who was with De Rohan. Hicks then took out a warrant for assault, thinking to detain the expedition long enough to compel the Government to take notice of our proceedings. The American sought refuge on board our steamer. I was the only member of the Committee at Harwich except the Secretary, Mr. G. J. Holyoake, who had gone to bed tired after his night's journey, so I had to take command of the steamer, sending Hicks' baggage ashore and refusing to let him come on board to search for the American. The policeman he brought alongside with him might come on board, but he might not, and the policeman not knowing the man, his quest would be in vain. The captain recognised me as master, and would take no orders but from me. There was a Government vessel in the harbour, but the captain of that was friendly with us, and when later in the day he came with Hicks I was willing to let the "Major" come on board to hunt for his man, by that time safely stowed away. In the afternoon De Rohan had to appear before the local magistrate, who imposed a fine of five shillings and came on board with us to supper and to talk of the Expedition. Late at night I went ashore again, to meet any men of the Legion who might have been delayed. One of those arriving was a Welsh parson who wanted to go as army chaplain, and was terribly disappointed when I told him there was no place for him. Letters came from the London Committee, which, our secretary being in bed, it was my business to read. One of them was from Sicily, appointing Hicks to the command of the Legion. I know not what interest he could have made to obtain this. I put the letter in my pocket, and going on board again waited till everybody had retired except De Rohan, then handed the letter to him. We kept our counsel. He appointed a military officer who was among those enrolled to the command of the Legion, and the next morning, the Legion fairly started, we left them, he to travel overland to reach Sicily before the expedition, I to report to the Committee, with whom I found a duplicate of the letter with Hicks' appointment, of course too late to be acted upon. Our judgment of the man had been right. The next I heard of him was his appearance in a police-court on some not creditable charge.

" *Grato in buoni servigi prestati dal Cap^{no.} De Rohan alla causa Italiana nelle campagne di Napoli e Sicilia,*
                              " G. GARIBALDI,"

was the Liberator's acknowledgment of De Rohan's services. The Legion arrived in Sicily too late to be much needed, except as an expression of British sympathy, but its behaviour was good and it was honourably reported.

Intimate with Mazzini, and devoted to him, De Rohan was his trusted envoy with Victor Emmanuel, whose respect and personal regard for Mazzini were very great, and who might have been influenced by him could there have been any escape from the influence of Cavour, whom the King for personal reasons held in dislike. " *Je déteste mon métier,*" the King said once to De Rohan; and on another occasion showed him "the only money I ever earned," money given to his majesty for some help rendered by him on one of his hunting excursions, when his dress had prevented his recognition.

I first met De Rohan on the Committee for this Sicilian Expedition. I admired him much, a distinguished-looking man, tall, well built, handsome, and possessing great strength, the *beau-idéal* of a sea king. We got to be very intimate; and years later he lived for months with me here at Hamden by New Haven. His business in the States was, being a naturalised American, to persuade the Government through Mr. Marsh, who was then American Minister at Rome, to press the Italian Government for payment of the three steamships chartered by De Rohan for Garibaldi's use, the said steamships having been drafted into the Italian navy. Time and patience were worn out in the delays and indifference of diplomacy, and no result obtained. The man who had generously given of his means, disappointed and weary, was not diplomatic; at last, on a visit to Rome, he personally offended the Italian Minister, and all chance of redress was lost. De Rohan died in poverty at Washington, and his three ships have not been paid for.

o

CHAPTER XXV

The Theatres; Charles Kemble; Macready; Braham; Pasta; Grisi
and Mario; Lablache; Straudigl; Schroeder Devrient; The
Keeleys; Mrs. Nesbitt; Mrs. Glover; Ellen Tree; Vestris; Tyrone
Power; Charlotte Cushman; Jefferson; Edwin Booth; Modjeska;
Amateur Acting; Barnard Gregory.

IN my young days I was very fond of the theatre,
not objecting to stint myself otherwise so as to
afford the pleasure of witnessing a good dramatic
performance or hearing a good singer. A week to
be particularly remembered was one in which I went
five nights to Covent-Garden to see the last acting
of Charles Kemble in his best characters — Hamlet,
Falconbridge in *King John*, Mark Antony in *Julius
Cæsar*, Mercutio in *Romeo and Juliet*, and Benedick
in *Much Ado about Nothing*. I have seen other
actors in these parts, from Macready to Irving, and
in America Edwin Booth; but the acting of Kemble,
old as he then was, has seemed to me to be unsur-
passed by any, my judgment perhaps influenced by
the recollection of my young enthusiasm. Braham,
old also, I heard once; and Pasta once; not in their
prime, but still great. Grisi and her husband Mario
I heard often, and beside their worth as singers remember that they were good Italians, friends of
patriotism and Mazzini. Great Lablache also I well

remember, and Staudigl in *Der Freischütz*, and Madame Schroeder Devrient, heard once in *Die Zauberflote*, and Adelaide Kemble in *Norma*. For the ballet I did not care. It seems to me that I never saw dancing worthy of the name, except that of Taglioni, none others that I thought graceful. Hers was the poetry of motion. During the time that I was editor of Hetherington's paper I had admission to several theatres. On the free list at Drury Lane under the management of Macready, I had only to sign my name to go in, for the whole of a play, or for half an hour or so as might please me. *Acis and Galatea* and Purcell's *King Arthur* were repeated pleasures, not only for sake of the music, but the drop scene to *Acis and Galatea* was one of Stanfield's masterpieces, aided by the illusion of the sea ripples coming up the beach; and in the *King Arthur* it was worth noting that by the simple arrangement of the army sufficiently occupying the stage to give time for returns from behind the scenes to follow on, there was the fair appearance of an army of thousands. It was but the adaptation of an old story of two men of equal height, and cloaked to appear alike, engaging a coach on a foggy night (a London fog), and when the coach stopped having both doors open, so that the first coming out had time to go behind the coach and reënter while the second leisurely descended, the first then passing out as a third occupant, the second in the same way appearing as a fourth, and the game continued till the poor driver thought his coach was haunted. It was perhaps the first time so very obvious an expedient was used on the stage, and it was very effective in the place of the three or four soldiers, "drum and colours," to be supposed an army. Macready was great in these scenic proprieties. Great also as an actor, but rather from close and wise study than from such fire of natural genius as must have marked the elder Kean. His Hamlet, his King John, his Lear, Shylock, Macbeth, Brutus and Julius Cæsar, Othello, and Benedick, were all excellent, if not at the topmost height. Certainly his Romeo was not equal to that of Edwin Booth, nor to that of Charlotte Cushman, who was the best Romeo I ever saw, though she startled us on her first appearance in the character in London, by her likeness to Macready. She gave me some friendly introductions when I came to America in 1866. Liston I can almost recall to sight, and John Reeve also, an admirable comic actor, sober or drunk, always master of himself before the footlights, though unsoberly not fit to appear the minute before. Admirable actors, too, were little Keeley and his wife, she a singer also, good in both capacities. I remember her especially as the Blind Girl of Portici, in Bulwer's *Last Days of Pompeii*. Then there was the bewitching Madame Vestris, the daughter of the famous engraver Bartolozzi, not beautiful, but fascinating, a fine actress and charming singer, great in her fairy tale Easter extravaganzas, and as great with the beautiful Mrs. Nesbitt in the *School for Scandal*, with Charles Matthews as Charles Surface. There was acting in those days,— the acting of Farren, and Harley, and Buckstone, and Miss P. Horton, who played the Fool in *Lear*, Mrs. Glover, Ellen Tree, Helen Faucit, and little Miss Poole, the most cat-like White Cat in one of Vestris' extravaganzas; and that most accomplished of Irishmen, Tyrone Power, who was drowned in the " President " ! The only actor I have ever seen to compare with him for thorough identification with his impersonation is Joseph Jefferson in the part of Rip Van Winkle. But in America I have had little opportunity, and not the same enthusiasm, for keeping up my love of the drama. Chiefly to be noted by me in these later days is Edwin Booth, whom I had the honour and pleasure of seeing occasionally both on and off the stage, free of his theatre during his first performances in the one built by him in New York, free to speak with him behind the scenes, and meeting him sometimes at the Century Club in New York ; a fine actor, a worthy gentleman, and an agreeable and attractive man.

The great Polish actress Madame Modjeska I saw but once on the stage; but I prize among my correspondence a letter from her thanking me for a number of the *Century Magazine*, which I sent to her because in an article on *European Republicans* it chronicled some of her compatriots.

Her letter is worth here giving :

NEW YORK, Jan. 20, 1888.

DEAR MR. LINTON:

I thank you most sincerely for the honour and kindness you have done to me in sending me a copy of *The Century* containing your beautiful article.

I should like to express to you equally my gratitude for the interest you take in the country of my birth and my heart, and for all the work you have done in its behalf; but words would only be idle. . . Poland has not many friends now; there is no political capital to be made nowadays by raising one's voice in her favour. Few friends, but true ones, does our cause count abroad, and the only reward for them to which we may point is the realisation of the hope you expressed in your letter, — the resurrection of Poland, in which our belief shall last as long as our belief in God, and in the final victory of right over might, of good over evil.

Please accept my deep felt regards, and believe me,

Respectfully yours,

HELENA MODJESKA.

Here I may tell how I narrowly escaped making my own *début* on the boards. Not that I presumed on any vocation that way, or that I had any ambition for histrionic fame. But the Institute of Fine Arts had projected an amateur performance at the St. James' Theatre, for some art-benefit, the intended performers to be members of the Institute. I forget what the principal play was to be, but there was in it a Yorkshire character which was appropriated to Topham (the water-colour painter), a Yorkshireman and likely, as was afterwards proved, to play the part successfully; but the afterpiece was to be *Bombastes Furioso*, — Franklin, a tall, personable Irishman, who affected a visage like that of Charles I., with a beard shaped accordingly, was to be the King, — and I, then slight and womanly-looking, with little whisker and no beard or moustache, was cast for Glumdalca, the one female character. I would look the part well enough, the speeches were not difficult, and I might manage the one song. However, in the course of discussion a dissension occurred. Cruikshank would have the acting broadly comic. Franklin and I insisted that as a burlesque it should be treated with perfect seriousness and in high heroic fashion. We were out-voted and so relinquished our parts. I think mine was taken by a professional actress. Cruikshank had great applause for his buffoonery, and the success of the whole performance set the example of similar amateur theatricals, in which Dickens afterwards took the lead.

One other theatrical matter of a very different kind I may here speak of. On a certain morning London streets were placarded with the following notice : —

"GENTLEMEN OF LONDON!

"Mr. Barnard Gregory, the editor of the *Satirist*, will appear to-night at Covent-Garden Theatre, in the character of

HAMLET."

The placard had been put out by the *Punch* contributors, the object sufficiently obvious: to oppose Gregory, who was notorious as a rascally blackmailer. John Leech called on me in the morning to tell me of their purpose and to ask me to go. Of course I went, and took a friend with me; and we got forward seats in the pit. Looking round, I saw a lot of rough fellows who, I concluded, were no doubt hired as *claqueurs* for Gregory, and was not without fear of a fierce conflict. The curtain drew up, and the action of the play began in all serenity; but so soon as Hamlet made his appearance an outcry, a burst of execration, rose so suddenly, and was so general, that one saw at once no opposition could make head against it. Hisses and hootings, cries of " Off! off!— Blackguard! scoundrel!" and the like were hurled at the actor; and the whole performance was stopped. Nothing was thrown except the storm of vociferation. Gregory faced it awhile, undauntedly impudent, then tried to make his voice heard in protest, but it was drowned in the roar of indignation. I was but three seats from the orchestra, and I could not hear a syllable of his speech though I saw his lips move. At length he gave in, and as the curtain came down he seemed to cower and crouch beneath. Then the manager came forward to withdraw the piece, and the conspirators went out to moisten their parched throats. Leech was hoarse for days. Lynch law, as it was, it was well deserved, though the man was, it was said, a promising actor. I forget what play was substituted, for a little while opposed by the minority who had come to support the Hamlet; but they had to give in, and the evening finished quietly.

One of those most active in the storm was the Duke of Brunswick, who had been grossly assailed in the *Satirist*. He had taken a stage box, from which he acted as fugleman to a party he had organised throughout the house, so giving us most unexpected help. Gregory brought an action against him for conspiracy. Jem Mace, a pugilist and publican living in the neighbourhood of the theatre, was, there was no doubt, one of those hired by the Duke, and prominently active. He was summoned as a witness, and did not deny the part he had taken, but denied having been hired for the conspiracy. He was asked: "What made you active in such a matter? what interest had you in it?" His interest, he replied, in public morality; he could not help protesting against such a man disgracing the stage — his words not these exactly, but to such purpose. The judge complimented him, and said he was glad to find so much public spirit in the parish in which he had his own residence.

CHAPTER XXVI

George Francis Train; Bunker Hill; Herbert Spencer; Voyage to New York; Cooper Institute; Peter Cooper; A. S. Hewitt; Dr. Rimmer; Frank Leslie; Squier; Cluseret; Pelletier; Aaron Powell; Wendell Phillips; The Fosters; Theodore Parker; Edmund Davis; Kentucky Lands; Colonisation in Montana; Frederick Douglas; Negro Bones.

GEORGE FRANCIS TRAIN I met in London. He was busy with endeavour to have cars employed on tramways in London streets. They became general enough in after time, but Train's immediate success was stopped by his running athwart some parochial interests which he did not care to consider. He used to invite " twelve live men " to breakfast with him on Sunday. I somehow got included in the invitations, but I did not go. I went however, once, to a midday public breakfast to meet some fifty or sixty men, most of them newspaper men or otherwise connected with literature, to commemorate the anniversary of the battle of Bunker Hill. Every one was expected to make a brief speech, not to exceed five minutes; and Train of course looked for sympathy with the North in the terrible fight then proceeding. I am sorry to say the company almost all had good words only for the South. A brother of Rudolph Lehman, the painter, and I were the

only two who spoke heartily for the North.   [It was
in such manner and from such men that the impression arose in America that the English people were
in favour of the South, — an impression very far
from correct : the feeling of the English people was
not with the South.   Even in the factory districts,
where the operatives were starving, out of work
because the supply of cotton was stopped, a public
meeting could not be had to express sympathy with
the slaveholders.]   The speeches over, Train, as host,
summed up, with no ill-taste or ill-feeling, very
fairly rating his guests ; then, turning pleasantly to
those remaining gathered round one table, impro-
vised in verse on each name in turn, finishing every
stanza with a popular American chorus.   It was
very clever, and well done.

Afterwards I met him in America.   I was to
breakfast with my friend De Rohan at the Fifth
Avenue Hotel, and entering the breakfast-room, we
stumbled upon Train, who was just finishing his
meal.   He knew De Rohan and promptly laid hold
of us, insisting that we should breakfast with or
beside him.   We soon had a group of listening
waiters at our end of the table.   Train was then
posing as a candidate for the Presidency, and told
us he was to lecture somewhere (I forget where) in
Broadway that evening — his hundredth, or hundred
and odd, lecture, canvassing for his election.   Having nothing better to do in the evening, I went to
the meeting.   He spoke fluently and well, though

with not much in his words. He had the platform to himself. During his speech he went to one end of the platform and, taking hold of his nose with one hand, ran across the platform to the other end, saying: "Let my nose alone! That," he added, "is the Democratic Party!" Then, taking his nose with the other hand, he ran back: "You, too, let my nose alone! That is the Republican Party. I don't mean to be led by the nose by either." Another time, after some sentiment, he said: "There's my friend Mr. Linton who will agree with that." Fortunately, he did not point at me; so I was able to turn round to see where his friend Linton might be sitting, and so escaped notice. The audience had to wait to shake hands with the "future President" as they went out.

Herbert Spencer, after his visit to America, was my fellow-voyager to England. I had pleasant talks with him, rather from him, when he was well enough to be on deck. He appeared to me a very full man, full of knowledge and sure of it, and not anxious for more from me, even if I had had it at his command, but I had not even on wood-engraving. I was more attracted to his friend, Mr. Lott, a Derby stock-broker, who had special care of him, at whose house in the neighbourhood of Derby I afterwards spent a glad evening and a morning.

In 1866 I had little occupation in England, and thought the opportunity good to see the new country, with no fixed intention of remaining. So in November of that year I crossed the ocean to New York, with nothing before me except a commission to write some letters of my American impressions for the Manchester *Examiner*, and with a few introductions from Dr. Wilkinson, Miss Cushman, my old friend Wehnert, and Mazzini. I was also strongly commended to the Temperance Party (though not belonging to them) by my friend Dr. Lees, the president of the party in England ; and I had business introductions from the Fullartons of Edinburgh, who had a business in New York before the war. These I had no occasion to use. Wehnert's letter took me to Dr. Rimmer, the master of the School of Design at the Cooper Institute. This brought me to acquaintance with Mr. Cooper, the philanthropic and venerable founder of the Institute, and with his son-in-law, Mr. Abram S. Hewitt, whose goodness I gratefully remember. They induced me to undertake for a time the teaching of the Wood Engraving Class at the Institute. Thought kindly of by the men of my profession, I had a supper given me by the Society of Wood Engravers, and was almost immediately taken hold of by Frank Leslie to work for his *Illustrated News*, and afterwards engaged by him to conduct the pictorial portion.

My welcome seemed a sufficient reason for my contemplating a longer stay in the States. I had only thought of remaining so long as might be necessary to organise a party for Italy, and to see something of the people and the country. But the object of these recollections is not to speak of myself, but to tell what little I can of the more remarkable personages whom I have known, and of events in which I have been concerned or with which I have been connected. Of the remarkable men, surely Peter Cooper was one. Not deferring to do good work by legacies, he, after making a fortune by his industry, nearly ruined himself in building and endowing the Institute, a reading-room and free schools for the working classes of New York City, asking only to have it remembered as the gift of " Peter Cooper, Mechanic, of New York." Both Mr. Cooper and Mr. Hewitt and their families were more than kind to me from my first acquaintance with them.

Dr. Rimmer, a notable man, was also very promptly my good friend. A good physician, and in good practice, the bent of his natural disposition took him to Art. Without model he sculptured in granite a life-sized head of St. Stephen; and afterwards executed a figure of a Dying Gladiator, so admirably that, when it was exhibited in Paris, it was at first declared to be modeled from life, but was indeed of too heroic size for that. As a teacher he was excellent, both in his school and as a lecturer, and on the black-board. A Swedenborgian and a poet, I had much pleasant and cordial intercourse with him, at the school, and among his family, at his and my own lodgings in New York, and once for a few days at his house in Chelsea, by Boston. He died within a couple of years of my coming to America.

"Frank Leslie,"—the name he took in America,—an English engraver, who had come, many years before, to the States, and after hard and persistent effort had succeeded in establishing a weekly illustrated newspaper in rivalry of Harper's, was also very kind to me and made me welcome to his house, in which Mr. and Mrs. Squier were living with him. Mrs. Squier, a beautiful and clever woman, was afterwards divorced from Squier, married Leslie, and since his death has conducted the paper. Leslie was a man ill-spoken of because for years he had been struggling and impecunious; but he had his good points, — some love of Art, though not an artist, and much kindness and generosity when he had means. I gave up my position on his paper after a brief holding because he also undertook another paper of a character I did not choose to be connected with. Ephraim G. Squier was a man who ought to have earned a good repute, a man of ability and abundant energy, who had been a great traveler in Peru, and whose conversation, when I could be alone with him and get him to talk of Peru, was very entertaining. Softening of the brain spoiled what should have been a life of much accomplishment.

My purpose to aid, if possible, the cause of Italy, and my known sympathy with the Abolitionist Party, brought me in contact with many men: with Cluseret and Pelletier on republican ground, with Aaron Powell and Wendell Phillips and the Fosters and Edmund Davis and others of the anti-slavery people. General Cluseret, a big Frenchman, with some talent as an artist, was much ill-spoken of in the New York *Tribune*, in other American papers, and in the *Fortnighty Review* in England, for his connection with the Fenians, but chiefly for being concerned with the Paris Commune, which the *Tribune* took special pains to confuse with Communism. Knowing him personally in New York, and with some tracking of his after course, I have no reason to think of him as other than a brave, earnest, chivalrous, and perhaps somewhat too hot-headed and self-opinionated republican, true to his party, if not always what I might think wise in his course. Claude Pelletier, by profession a printer, of Lyons, who had been member for Lyons in the French Constituent Assembly, in the brief republican interregnum after the Revolution of '48, the friend of Pierre Leroux and Ledru Rollin, was exiled from France by the Empire. After some sojourn in England he came to New York. For a living he engaged himself as a cook at a restaurant, and so occupied himself till he had saved money enough to bring his wife and two sons over, and to go into business as an artificial florist. A good republican, good in himself, well-informed, indeed of wide knowledge, an excellent writer, he left, only part printed, when he died, a *Dictionary of Socialism* after the method of Voltaire's *Philosophical Dictionary*. He was also author of a revolutionary drama — *Le Savetier de Messine* (the Cobbler of Messina) — of considerable merit.

Cluseret and Pelletier I knew from the time of my arrival; Aaron Powell, the editor of the *Anti-Slavery Standard*, also, and from my first knowledge of him he only grew in my esteem as one of the most single-hearted and liberal-minded men I have ever met with: a liberal Quaker, and liberal albeit in his practice a strict temperance man, with a gentle-natured wife worthy of him. He introduced me to Wendell Phillips at one of the many meetings which were still being held continuously, in order to make sure that the emancipation of the coloured people should be fairly carried out. At this particular meeting Phillips had to take the chair, and asked me to wait till after the meeting he came out of the committee-room. I did so. He came out with friends around him, warmly grasped my hand and held it as we went down the steps at the entrance of the hall, then leading me to dinner with him at the St. Denis Hotel. The same heartiness always greeted me whenever we met, whether at a public meeting where, more than once, I had the honour of speaking from the same platform, or at the gatherings of the Radical Club at the Rev. Mr. Sargent's in Boston, or in his own house when I called upon him. A man with a commanding presence, dignified in manner, with a frank look, and a benignant smiling mouth, from which one would no more expect sarcasm or invective than lightning from the clear sky. Fierce indeed could be his denunciations of wrong, the utterances of a Jove, but a Jove who could be

P

jovial, in all the familiar meaning of that word. I have heard no orator with such various power, language so ready and so choice, calm and convincing in argument, or overwhelming all opposition with the torrent of his vehement passion. His opponents must have admired him; his friends could not help but love him. I was proud of the distinction of finding myself counted among the last.

Theodore Parker must have been a man of the same stamp. I only knew him by his printed sermons, some of which he sent to me in England. Some I reprinted. When he passed through London on his way to Italy, a brief while before his death, I missed seeing him by half an hour, to my great regret. Garrison, also, I never saw; but I had some correspondence with him through and in the *Liberator*, which before I left England he used to send to me.

Among the best of the Abolitionist Party that I knew were Abby Kelly Foster and Stephen Foster, her husband: Mrs. Foster a little, frail-looking woman, but full of energy and the calmness of a never-failing courage. At a certain meeting at which I was present, her tall, more impulsive husband insisted on pressing a motion for some question of woman's rights which, considering the purpose of the meeting, was quite out of order. Impatient at his persistency, I thought to myself, O that some woman would answer him. At last he sat down, and it was his wife who rose to reply. Very quietly, with better logic, she put him fairly out of court. But it was done with perfectly good taste and kindly, womanly feeling, the most satisfactory setting down that could be, whether for matter or manner, and the good husband, in spite of his opinion, must have been pleased with as well as proud of her. Once at a lecture upon Abraham Lincoln, given by Emerson at the Radical Club in Boston, his praise of Lincoln seemed to me too exclusive, and, as each of the audience was asked to make some brief comment on the lecture, I ventured to suggest that John Brown should have place of honour beside the President. Mr. Foster, who spoke next, supported me. Among these best of American nobles whom I have known I must not forget Robert Purvis of Philadelphia, a man of dignified bearing, though with, I believe, negro blood in his veins, as handsome and aristocratic in appearance as the Irish patriot, Wm. Smith O'Brien, and of as chivalrous a character. Neither must I forget Edmund Davis, also of Philadelphia, the husband of a daughter of Lucretia Mott. I had to know a great deal of him, being at one time his agent in London, endeavouring to procure a purchaser for a hundred thousand acres of land in Kentucky, between the Cumberland River and the Tennessee border, near to Cumberland Gap, in the Cumberland Mountains, where some day may be a great central city. With an artist friend and a young engineer, I went there to report, especially on the coal, and spent a week or more prospecting the land, camping out where we could. I was led to undertake the agency for Davis from being baulked in a scheme for bringing out an English colony (which I hoped to make a republican nucleus) to Montana, — baulked by the failure of Jay Cooke and consequent deferral of the North Pacific Railroad.

Frederick Douglas, the coloured orator, a natural orator, I heard once at a meeting in New York. Several other coloured men, estimable, if not so notable, I have become acquainted with at public meetings and in private; and learned from them to believe in the possibility of their race yet playing a part in the world's history, outgrowing the disqualifications natural or consequent on generations of slavery. I was once at a coloured ball at Washington, and could observe no difference but that of colour from the balls of society of the best of our middle classes. I have hope of the race, notwithstanding the judgment of a very gentlemanly and I doubt not competent Southern editor, who assured me that the negro's configuration, even to his bones, is anatomically different from that of the white man, a creature indeed differing so essentially that, if Mr. Darwin's theory be right, he must have proceeded from a very inferior ape.

CHAPTER XXVII

American Poets; Bryant; Stedman; Stoddard; Mrs. Stoddard; Bayard Taylor; Lowell; Longfellow; Whittier; Emerson; Alcott; Whitman; Mrs. Howe; Anthony; Bret Harte; Whipple; Fremont; Agassiz; Other Notables; Tilden; Madame Blavatsky; A. T. Stewart; Cespedes and Cuba; General Butler; Sumner; Anderson; Adams; Page.

WITH the poets of America I have had very pleasant opportunities. Bryant was President of the Century Club, the best of clubs in New York or anywhere (though I did not please Sir Richard Temple by saying so when we encountered on our voyage to England), of which I had the honour and gratification of becoming a member almost immediately after my arrival in New York. Richard Henry Stoddard and Edmund Clarence Stedman, also members of the Century, have been from soon after my arrival in America to this day my valued friends; Stoddard, indeed, a very close, I may say an intimate, friend, with whom I never fail to spend as much as possible of my time whenever I have occasion to visit New York, for meetings of the Century or otherwise. Stoddard I believe to be the highest poetic genius now living in America, his work always good, always of the very highest character. His wife, Mrs. Elizabeth Barstow Stoddard, has not written much verse, but what she has written would not be unworthy of her husband, and she is known as a clever novelist. Their friendship counts among my great gains. Bayard Taylor I met frequently at the Club. To Lowell I was introduced at the University Press, in Cambridge, Massachusetts, and had pleasant words from him afterwards. Longfellow, whom I met at the same most excellent of printing offices, then conducted by Welch, Bigelow & Co., took me home with him to his house in Cambridge, and gave me very cordial welcome. Whittier I met at the Sargents' (Mr. Sargent was the clergyman who first dared to admit Theodore Parker to his pulpit; and he and his wife were the centre of the abolitionists and other liberal people in Boston). I had a letter from Whittier when for an American anthology (which I was editing with Stoddard) I wrote to him to ask the date of his birth: a letter from him strangely contradicting the generally, I may say the universally, received belief in the date of that day. He wrote to me : —

> "BEAR CAMP RIVER HOUSE,
> "West Ossipee, N. H.
> "13, 9 mo., 1875.

"MY DEAR SIR:

"My birthday was the very last of the year 1807.

"I remember with pleasure meeting thee at the Radical Club meeting at Mr. Sargent's some two or three years ago.

"I am stopping here for a month at a pleasant old inn among the mountains, in the hope to recruit my health. The weather is delightful. We seem both engaged somewhat similarly. I am making a *small* collection of English & American Poets of the last 3 centuries.

> " Very truly thy friend,
> "J. G. WHITTIER."

To Emerson I brought an introduction from Dr. Garth Wilkinson. I was in the back room of the book-store of Messrs. Ticknor & Fields, Boston (who as publishers held much the same position with the American poets as Moxon held with English, and at whose daily lunch one met the best of literary men in Boston), when Emerson came into the store. Mr. Ticknor asked me — Would I like to see him? "Most certainly; also I had a letter for him." He came in, read the letter (the introduction which Dr. Wilkinson had given me), shook hands with me, and asked — Was I staying in Boston? If so, I must come out to Concord next day to dine with him. I regretted that I could not do so, as I had already an engagement for the morrow, and at Concord. "With whom?" I told him with the Austens (Mrs. Austen, a novelist of considerable repute, but lately dead, whom I had met and admired at New York). "You will dine then with me." I found my friends next day engaged to take me with them to Emerson's. He and Mrs. Emerson and their daughter Ellen were all very cordial and attentive. Emerson showed me his several photographs of Carlyle, and spoke to me of my friends the Scotts, David and William, speaking admiringly of William's poem, the *Year of the World*, on account of its unwonted truth to Indian thought and theosophy. He inquired for the author of some paper in *Punch*, which had interested him; and there was some talk about printers' blunders. He said they were not always in the wrong. He had an instance when once he had used the expression, "going up a declivity." His printer suggested "acclivity." Said Emerson, "I did not know the word, and I had thought that if I could go down a declivity I could also go up." His printer, Mr. Bigelow, of the University Press, told me afterwards the same story as an instance of Emerson's receptiveness. The next time I was in Concord of course I called. The family were all away. I offered my card to the Irish servant. "And what will I be doing with this?" she asked as she looked at it. I said, "Give it to Mr. Emerson when he comes home!" "I guess I'll give it to Miss Ellen." "I dare say that will do," I rejoined. There was no assumption of style about the Emerson family; they were simply well-bred, cultured gentlefolk, not fashionable people. In his later days Emerson's voice failed him for lecturing, and still later and more entirely his memory of words. His hesitation for the right word had to be met by guesses. At Longfellow's grave, having to speak of him, very touching was the failure — "Our dear friend, whose name at this moment I can not recall." At Concord I saw and spoke with Bronson Alcott, a strange, mystical, gentle old philosopher, very gracious, very wordy, rather incomprehensible. I have some vague remembrance of having, very early in England, met a tall, slight, gentle dreamer, Charles Lane, a somewhile partner and associate of Alcott.

Walt Whitman I first saw at his desk in the Treasury at Washington. Afterwards I called on him at his home (his brother's house) in Camden, over the river from Philadelphia. And I had some friendly correspondence and interchange of writings with him. I liked the man much, a fine-natured, good-hearted, big fellow, who must have been handsome in young days (as indeed an early portrait shows him); a true poet who could not write poetry, much of wilfulness accounting for his neglect of form, perhaps as fatal a mistake in a poet as in a painter. He was great, and greatly esteemed, as a volunteer nurse with the armies of the North during the war. They say that a regiment once presented arms to him in recognition of his honourable service and benevolent ministrations; and that Lincoln especially pointed him out for his noble work.

Of many other notabilities, more or less notable, I can only speak as having met them a few times, or it might be only once, without much impress from them. Mrs. Julia Ward Howe, the author of the *Battle Hymn of the Republic*, the best war-lyric of the time of the conflict between North and South, the wife of Dr. Howe, the good physician of the deaf and dumb, I met occasionally in Boston. Aldrich, poet, I used to meet in Boston at the house of my friend Anthony, a brotherly brother wood-engraver. At his house, too, I dined once with Bret Harte and with Whipple, the clever essayist. I spoke with General Fremont once on the floor of the House of Representatives at Washington ; Agassiz I heard lecture in New York ;

Oliver Wendell Holmes I met once at the Century; John Fiske I at times met there, and Clarence King, and Professors Peirce and Pumpelly, and the Rev. Robert Collyer, and many others of equal estimation: among them the most genial of Irishmen, Chief Justice Daly, whom I may call my friend. Tilden one evening came out with me from Peter Cooper's. His house in Gramercy Park (next to that now occupied by the Players' Club) was close by, and, though late at night, he took me in to show me certain books in his library. Madame Blavatsky and the dry-goods *millionnaire*, A. T. Stewart, I happened once to catch sight of in the studio of Le Clear, who was painting Stewart's portrait. One sight of Madame was enough, a fat, vulgar-looking woman, not, one could not help thinking, at all likely to be mistaken for a prophetess, no sibyl but a veritable old witch, with nothing venerable about her. There is a story of a Jew who, putting his son to school, was so particular in his directions that it could not but be remarked that he had said nothing about the lad's religious instruction. Reminded of it, he replied, " Well, I think a North of Ireland Presbyterian is the man to make most money, bring him up to that." Stewart was a North of Ireland Presbyterian of that stamp. When he began business in New York, he had to put up his own shutters at night and carry home his own parcels of goods sold during the day, not even keeping an errand-boy. When he had his two immense white marble dry-goods stores, wholesale and retail, and his marble palace on Fifth Avenue, it is said that he still coveted the business of small traders in the poorer districts. He looked the character. Surely it was a sort of poetic justice that ordered the stealing of his body, so to prevent his burial in the costly cenotaph he had built for himself. Of good-natured Horace Greeley, the " self-made man who worshiped his Creator," I had only a passing glimpse one day as he rushed out of the *Tribune* Office to catch a street-car.

General Ben Butler and the great Massachusetts Senator, Charles Sumner, I saw and spoke with at sundry times. Cespedes' brave attempt for the freedom of Cuba, for its deliverance from Spain and for the emancipation of the slaves, had a promise of success. And perhaps had not failed had Grant conceded belligerent rights, as he had promised to Rawlings. Rawlings dead, the promise was not kept. This was but a little while after my arrival in America. I was led to interest myself in the Cuban struggle by Cluseret and another republican friend, Dr. Basora, a physician practising in New York. Basora was born in one of the West Indian Islands, his father a slaveholder there. When the father died, he left a large estate ; but the son, then a young man, disdained to hold his fellow-men in bondage, and refused his inheritance. He was active in the Cuban cause. Strongly sympathising, I gave what help I could by writing for it ; and when they wanted an American General, I was asked to see General Butler

and get him to name a man good for the purpose.
Butler gave me an introduction to one whom he
recommended as a brave and daring and capable man,
who had served under him. I called upon the man
in Boston, and found him to be, instead of the
expected fierce, grim warrior, a quiet-looking, smooth-
faced, gentlemanly man, who "regretted," and
seemed sincerely to regret, that he had settled down
since the war as a man of peace, begun business as a
lawyer, and could not be disturbed again. Butler,
who was very courteous to me and obliging, was a
man to remember: not tall but portly, with a magnificent head which, if you were looking down from
the gallery to the House of Representatives, at Washington, you would be attracted to, not merely for its
baldness, but as the head of certainly a man of intellect and ability. He had a good face, too, in spite of
a curious obliquity in one eye, concerning which a
good story is told. He was cross-examining a witness, and browbeating him. The culmination of his
repeated questions was "Will you look me in the
eye and swear to this?" "In which eye? General!"
was the retort. Butler had bitter enemies, not un-
deserved if reports be true that he was not only harsh
as military governor at New Orleans, but that he
was also extortionate, making no scruple of feathering
his nest in the conquered city. Yet there was the
praise for him that while he was in command there,
New Orleans, owing to his sanatory strictness, was
free from yellow fever. Sumner, a large, handsome

man, with courteous manner, I had also to see on some Cuban business, and was very graciously received. His home in Washington was like a museum, full of statuettes and rare engravings.

So many artists were members of the Century Club that I soon had a wide artistic acquaintance. A closer brotherhood among artists appears to me to obtain in New York than in London ; and the generous feeling was liberally extended to myself. I helped in founding the Society of Painters in Water-colour in New York ; was admitted as an Associate of the National Academy of Design, and in due time was elected a full member. It might seem invidious to name individuals among those whom I knew when first here, twenty-seven years ago, many since dead, and those of to-day whom I may still call friends, but I may signalise two of the gone, because men of my own profession as engravers, and both men of mark, — Anderson and Adams.

Alexander Anderson, born in 1775, is worthy of notice as the first engraver in wood in the United States of America. His father being a copper-plate printer, the boy became acquainted with Hogarth's and other prints, and soon had an ambition to try his own hand. He was only twelve years old when he got a silversmith to roll out some copper cents ; then he himself made a graver of the back spring of a pocket-knife, and so started as an amateur engraver in copper. After a while, a blacksmith made some tools for him, and he began to engrave in relief little cuts of ships, houses, and the like, for newspaper advertisements, becoming known for such work and earning money by it. His father, however, having little faith in the business, placed him with a physician, and, at the age of twenty, he was licensed to practise on his own account, and for three years did practise with considerable distinction. In 1798 the yellow fever was in New York, and Anderson's wife and infant son, his father and mother, his brother, and some other kin-folk, fell victims to it. With no heart left for an active life, he retired into the quiet seclusion of an engraver's work, which, indeed, he had never entirely abandoned. The early delight became his solace, his sole occupation, and, industriously followed, both in incised work and relief, in copper and type-metal, and afterwards in wood, gave him a living and reputation. In 1802 he undertook the reproduction of Bewick's *Quadrupeds*, three hundred cuts for an American edition. They were admirable copies, only reversed. Other engravings by him, most of them copies from English work, are of equal fidelity, though he had no genius in design and even as an engraver was hardly to be called great. The esteem of his contemporaries was shown by his election as an honorary member of the National Academy of Design in New York, in 1843. I visited him at Williamsburg in 1867, soon after my first coming to America, and found him a hale old man of ninety-two, with his graver in his hand, pleasing himself with being still at work. I believe he was "at work" to within a few days of his death, on the 17th of January, 1870, in the ninety-fifth year of his age.

Joseph Alexander Adams, born in 1803, came to meet me at a supper given to me on occasion of my arrival in New York at the end of 1866, by the Society of Wood Engravers. I had the pleasure of meeting him occasionally afterwards, and also had correspondence with him, enabling me to give account of his life and works in my *History of Wood Engraving in America*, published by Estes & Lauriat, Boston, in 1882. I had also from him the friendly gift of a number of his best proofs now safely preserved in the Museum of Fine Arts at Boston, Mass. Self-taught in engraving like Anderson, he was likewise a careful art-student, sufficiently accomplished to be elected an Associate of the National Academy of Design, though when I there inquired concerning him I could learn nothing of him. Having withdrawn from Art, his name had somehow been dropped from the Academical list. I recollect seeing his work even during my own apprenticeship. He was in England in 1831, and already could show work which might fairly compare with the best of a similar character of our great engraver, John Thompson. Here in America he was most known for sixteen hundred engravings from drawings by J. G. Chapman, in Harper's Bible (1843), which, however, are nearly all the work of his pupils. The profits of that book gave him means for travel and a competence for life. He spent nearly eight years in Europe, and returning home, gave up Art and applied himself to scientific pursuits. Adams' most excellent hand-press is of his invention.

One other name, that of William Page, sometime President of the National Academy of Design, must yet be chronicled, not only because of the esteem in which his memory is held by his fellow-artists and my own admiration of the painter's art, in which he was singularly great, but also out of love of the man for his rich and generous nature. I had the happiness of being very much in his company and in very close friendship with him, and I regretted his death as I would that of a very dear elder brother.

CHAPTER XXVIII

Late Years; British Museum; Austin Dobson; Excursions; Paris and Oxford; B. F. Stevens; Closing Words.

IN very latest years, during several visits to England, I had the satisfaction of adding new friends to the friends of old time still living. Among the old were my oldest friend, W. B. Scott, who during my last visit was sick at Penkill Castle in Ayrshire; my good old physician and friend, Dr. Philip Brown, still in practice at Blaydon but residing near by, at Wylam on Tyne; my three Brantwood helpers on the *English Republic*, all holding affectionately to me; my old pupil, Walter Crane; other old pupils, and several of my fellow-engravers, who retained their old regard, notably two who sat beside me in days of apprenticeship. I may call an old friend Dr. George Bullen, the genial and ever courteous keeper of the Printed Books at the British Museum, as I had reason to know him in very early days when I was a reader at the Library; but in later visits had to know more of him, and to be more and more indebted to him for his unstinted help. For such help also I had to be indebted to Dr. Garnett, who on Dr. Bullen's retirement took his place in the Museum. As principals

Q   225

there I can but speak prominently of them ; but the same friendly help was rendered me through many years by Mr. Reid, keeper of the Prints, and afterwards by Professor Colvin, who succeeded him ; and indeed by every one connected with the Museum, Library, and Print Room during the years in which I was engaged in researches for *The Masters of Wood Engraving*, or for a collection of *English Verse* (published in five volumes by Messrs. Scribner of New York), for which my friend, R. H. Stoddard, wrote the Introductions in each volume. The *English Verse* brought me into some correspondence, for leave to publish in England, with Browning, Swinburne, Buchanan, and other English poets. Buchanan I met once at the Century in New York. Arthur J. Munby I met at Scott's, before Scott left Chelsea for Ayrshire, and I had the pleasure of meeting him several times beside. I had the pleasure, too, of friendly intercourse with Austin Dobson, whose charming verse and prose reflect the cheerful, genial nature of the man. Here I can not resist the temptation to insert some lines by him, written on the fly-leaf of his *Thomas Bewick and his Pupils*, which he sent to me in 1884, dedicating the book to me as " Engraver and Poet, the steadfast apostle of Bewick's white line " :

> " Not white thy graver's path alone ;
>   May the sweet Muse with whitest stone
>   Mark all thy days to come, and still
>   Delay thee on Parnassus Hill.
>
>   " AUSTIN DOBSON."

The white line refers of course to the peculiar method of engraving followed by Bewick and his best pupils, Clennell and Nesbit, and which, my life through, I have sought to maintain, as the only artistic method of engraving in wood.

I was in England at the end of 1867, and went to Paris to the Exposition; again in England in 1872–3; again in the latter part of 1882, during 1883 and the first half of 1884, and again at the close of 1887, through the whole of 1888 and 1889, and to the end of May, 1890. During these last two visits I made several excursions, twice for a few days' stay with my friend W. J. Hennessy, the American painter, at St. Germain, near Paris, and during my last visit twice for a few days with W. B. Scott, in Ayrshire; once to my Brantwood printer at Cheltenham; once to my good old Dr. Brown at Wylam; once to Earl Spencer's library at Althorp, near Northampton; twice to Oxford, for the first time with my friend Arthur Bullen, the able editor of Elizabethan Lyrics, the son of Dr. Bullen of the Museum, the second as the guest of Mr. C. J. Firth, each time having the opportunity of seeing the old halls, more than once dining in hall. "See Venice and die!" says the proverb, and an Englishman should not die without some acquaintance with the venerable beauty of Oxford.

Coming to England in 1882, I brought an introduction from Mrs. Page, the wife of the painter, to her two Vermont brothers, Henry Stevens, the Bible bibliographer, and Benjamin Franklin Stevens, the Despatch Agent of the United States in London. By both (Mr. Henry is since dead) I was most friendlily received. More than ordinary friendliness I had from Mr. B. F. Stevens when I again came to England in October, 1887. For some months I was his guest at his home in Surbiton, and to his wise counsel and generous help I owe the being able to produce and bring out the work for which I had been for many years preparing material, and which resumes all I would care to say on my own art,— *The Masters of Wood Engraving*. Probably it is for this book that the neighbouring (in New Haven) University of Yale has honoured me by conferring on me the degree of Master of Arts.

During twenty-seven years, since I first came to America, I have had constant experience of kindly regard for me as an Englishman, not merely on personal grounds, and rejoicingly I seem to perceive everywhere a growing attachment to the Old Country, which I believe to be heartily reciprocated. I close these recollections, not at all written as an autobiography, with the hope that I may not be without some influence, however small, in promoting this good feeling between the two peoples, whose good understanding and close alliance is of so much importance to the world's welfare and progress. I would fain hope that I have not failed to do what little lay in my power as a man's duty toward the land I have so long lived in, though loyalty to the place of my birth has forbidden my becoming an American citizen. In young days I believed that an Englishman was bound to help not only toward the freedom and welfare of his own country, but toward the freedom and welfare of the world. I have not lost that belief, nor given up my faith that republicanism has yet to be the universal rule, the republicanism not merely of a mere unkingliness or of democratic and anarchical self-seeking, but the only true republicanism of a generous recognition of equality of rights and the fraternal exercise of religious duty.

HAMDEN BY NEW HAVEN, CONN., U. S. A.
Feb. 20, 1894.

INDEX

Lablache, 194.

Lamennais, 26, 104, 105, 121.

Lance (George), 73.

Landor (W. S.), 17, 124 to 126, 156, 157.

Landseer (T.), 177.

Lane (Charles), 216.
(Richard), 179.

Larken (Rev. E.), 119, 122.

Lausanne, 120, 121.

Laws against the Press, 27, 28.

Leader (The), 119, 122, 123.

Leader (John Temple), 33, 34.

Ledru Rollin, 142, 143, 146, 150.

Leech (John), 56, 58, 59, 60.

Lees (Dr. F. R.), 124, 139.

Legend of Florence, 38.

Leigh (Percival), 58, 59, 60.

Leitch (W. L.), 56, 73, 81.

Leslie (Frank), 205, 207.

Letter-Opening, 50 to 53.

Lewes (G. H.), 117, 122, 123.

Lietch (Dr.), 130.

Linnell (John), 181, 182.

Little Ease, 12.

Lloft (Capel), 173.

London Bridge, 12.

London Stone, 13.

London Working Men's Association, 32 to 34.

Longfellow (H. W.), 214.

Lott (Edward), 204.

Lotteries, 4.

Lover (S.), 174.

Lovett (William), 34, 37, 40, 50.

Lowell (J. R.), 214.

Macaulay (T. B.), 52.

Mace (Jem), 201.

Mackay (Charles), 57, 171.

Macready (W. C.), 38, 195, 196.

Martineau (Harriet), 168, 169.
(Rev. James), 139.

Matthews (Charles), 197.

Mayhew (Henry), 58.

Mazzini, 49 to 52, 98, 101, 103, 142 to 147, 151, 152, 153, 189.

Meadows (Kenny), 55, 56, 72.

Meagher's Letters, 108.

Medical Friends, 130, 131.

Medici (Colonel), 170.

Mediums, 169.

Millais (J. E.), 176.

Misrepresentations, 110 to 114.

Mitchell (Young), 73, 184.

Miteside, 78, 97, 118, 119.

Modjeska (Madame), 197, 198.

Monmouth Arms, 94.

Montgomery (Rev. R.), 174.

Moore (Richard), 30, 34, 37, 100.

Morgan (Lady), 60.
(Minter), 119.

Moxon (Edward), 87, 128, 129.

Mulready, 53.

Munby (A. J.), 226.

Mutual Instruction Society, 76.

Nation (The), 107, 124.

National (The, A Library for the People), 75.

National Union of the Working Classes, 32.

Nelson's Funeral, 4.

Nesbitt (Mrs.), 197.

Newman (F. W.) 159, 160.
J. H.), 160.

Northern Star (The), 35.

Oastler (Richard), 157.

O'Brien (Bronterre), 42.
(William Smith), 108, 211.

O'Connell (Daniel), 33, 34, 156.

O'Connor (Feargus), 35, 43.

Odd-Fellow (The), 37, 75.

Orion, 20